drama
SKITS & SKETCHES

THE *ideas* LIBRARY

FOR YOUTH GROUPS

The Ideas Library

drama SKITS & SKETCHES

THE 'ideas LIBRARY

FOR YOUTH GROUPS

Youth Specialties

ZondervanPublishingHouse
Grand Rapids, Michigan
A Division of HarperCollinsPublishers

Project editor: Vicki Newby
Cover design: Curt Sell
Interior design: Curt Sell and PAZ Design Group
Art director: Mark Rayburn

Printed in the United States of America

01 02 03 04 05 06 / VG / 15 14 13 12 11 10 9 8

CONTENTS

ALPHABETICAL LIST

TOPICAL INDEX TO SCRIPTS

Looking for a skit or drama for your meeting on faith? Friendship? Values and priorities? The will of God? Salvation? Simply glance down the list of topics and find the perfect script for your purpose and for your group. (Few of the "Just for Fun" skits are indexed here, because—well, they're just for fun and pretty much without topics per se.)

JUST
FOR FUN

Some of these skits are long; some are short. Some require little or no prep at all, and others involve memorizing scripts. All of them scream for performers who aren't afraid to ham it up. The more the actors put into their performances, the bigger the laughs they'll get.

THE GREATEST SHOW ON EARTH

The 56 puns in this skit on page 12 are guaranteed to bring 56 groans. *Chris Herpolsheimer*

HOT DOG

Want a comic illustration of misunderstanding? In this monolog it's a mixup between hot dogs and—well, canine dogs. The script is on page 16. *Graham Sowers*

MONK MONOTONY

An old joke that still pulls laughs from young crowds. *J. Russell Matzke*

CHARACTERS
    Abbot
    Monk Monotony
    A sign carrier

PROPS
    Large sign that reads TEN YEARS LATER

Ask the audience to imagine a monastery where Monk Monotony has just taken a vow of silence.

ABBOT: So, Monk Monotony, you have just taken a vow of silence?

(Monk Monotony shakes head yes)

ABBOT: Do you know what this vow of silence means?

(Monk Monotony shakes head yes)

The Greatest Show on Earth

CHARACTERS
•Announcer •Boss Leland, owner of the Big Top Circus •Bobo the Clown, Leland's assistant
•Bill Blade •Electro, the Human Wall Socket •Nelson Fury, the Human Bullet
•Barney Tomb, the Modern Mummy •Creepy Terry Tiptoe, the Tightrope Terror

ANNOUNCER: Boss Leland's Big Top Circus has just arrived in the small country town of Grissle. Boss now attempts to organize his troupe of performers. He calls for his best friend and trusty sidekick, Bobo the Clown.

BOSS: Bobo, come here. Do you have any idea what Grissle is like?

BOBO: I hear it's a pretty tough town.

BOSS: Really? I find that awfully hard to swallow. Bobo, this year's circus schedule is very demanding. I'm afraid we're going to have to limit the number of acts we have. Some of the ones we have now will have to go. I wrote up a list of doubtfuls. I want you to get Bill Blade and bring him here. I want to talk to him about his knife act.

ANNOUNCER: So Bobo brings Bill Blade to Boss. *(Bobo and Bill enter)*

BOSS: Well, well, Bill, don't you look sharp today.

BILL: You wanted to see me, Boss?

BOSS: Yes, I do.

BILL: It's about my knife act, isn't it?

BOSS: I'm afraid so. Face it, Bill, your knife act just doesn't cut it around here anymore.

BOBO: Yeah. It always was a bit dull.

BILL: I get the point—you don't think I can hack it. Well, I admit I'm a bit rusty, but I still have an edge on the other performers.

BOSS: I'm sorry, Bill, I've tried to carve you into a competent circus star, but you haven't done well with your job. No matter how you slice it, it's time for you to switch, Blade.

ANNOUNCER: So Bill Blade sadly leaves his circus home. *(Bill exits, weeping)*

BOBO: I think your words pierced his heart.

ANNOUNCER: Boss now calls in his next candidate on the list of doubtfuls, Electro, the Human Wall Socket. *(Electro enters)*

BOSS: Electro, I want to talk to you about something.

ELECTRO: Really, Watt?

BOSS: I have some bad news for you.

ELECTRO: If it's about last month's electric bill, I can explain...

BOSS: No, it's nothing to do with that. This may come as a shock to you, but I'm pulling the plug on your act.

ELECTRO: But why? I've only been here a few weeks. Couldn't you give me an extension?

BOSS: It's out of the question.

ELECTRO: You can't get rid of me that way. I've got connections!

BOSS: Now don't blow a fuse. You've traveled the whole circuit with us, but due to the current situation, I've got to disconnect you from the Big Top Circus.

ELECTRO: But I'm the highlight of the show!

BOSS: Go fly a kite.

ANNOUNCER: So Electro also sadly leaves his circus home. *(Electro exits)*

BOBO: He never was very bright.

BOSS: Who's next on the list?

BOBO: Nelson Fury, the Human Bullet.

BOSS: He's probably in the powder room. Bring him in. It should be fairly easy to fire the Bullet.

ANNOUNCER: So Bobo, Boss's best buddy, brings Bullet.

BOSS: Hello, Nelson.

NELSON: Hi Boss. You want to talk to me?

BOSS: Yes, it's about your act.

NELSON: My act? Has it triggered something in your mind?

BOSS: Not exactly, Nelson. I realize that you are a big shot around here, but I'm letting you go.

NELSON: But why? My act has always been loaded with excitement. Everyone says it's a barrel of laughs.

BOSS: Be reasonable. Surely a man of your caliber can understand. I've always gotten a big bang out of your act, but you'll have to find a new job somewhere else.

NELSON: I hate to be such a revolver. Shoot!

ANNOUNCER: And so the Human Bullet leaves the Big Top forever. *(Nelson exits)*

BOSS: Well, that's the last we'll see of him.

BOBO: The old son-of-a-gun.

ANNOUNCER: Suddenly Bobo is handed some dreadful news!

BOBO: Boss, I've been handed some dreadful news!

BOSS: What is it?

BOBO: Barney Tomb, the Modern Mummy, is quitting our circus!

BOSS: What? Bring him here. I want my Mummy!

ANNOUNCER: So Bobo brings the Modern Mummy to Boss.

(Bobo and Barney enter)

BOSS: What's this I hear about you quitting?

BARNEY: That's right. I'm getting tired of all this.

BOSS: You're kidding.

BARNEY: No, I'm dead serious.

BOSS: You're always so wrapped up in your work. Maybe you need a vacation to unwind a little bit. You'd feel a lot better.

BARNEY: No, I'm tired of being buried in responsibility. And my health...I'm coffin all the time.

BOSS: Where did you dig up that excuse?

BARNEY: This is a grave situation, Boss. Don't take it lightly. This circus routine bores me stiff.

BOSS: I can't help it if things have been a little dead lately.

BARNEY: Don't try shoveling the blame on someone else, Boss. Goodbye!

ANNOUNCER: And Barney the Modern Mummy angrily stomps out of the circus. *(Barney exits)*

BOBO: His act never was very lively.

BOSS: Who's next on our list?

BOBO: Creepy Terry, the Tightrope Terror. I'll go get him.

ANNOUNCER: So Creepy Terry, the Tightrope Terror, tiptoes in to see the Boss. *(Terry tiptoes in)*

TERRY: Hi Boss. What's up?

BOSS: Terry, I'm afraid your tightrope act is going to take a fall.

TERRY: You're pulling my leg.

BOSS: We're having trouble balancing the budget, and you've been getting out of line lately.

TERRY: That's a lie! I've always been a steady worker. Wire you doing this to me?

BOSS: We're tired of stringing you along.

TERRY: But Boss, I've always walked the line! And don't forget that I've got friends in high places!

BOSS: Sorry, Terry, you're out! We're tired of you acting like you were above us all.

TERRY: I'm a level-headed guy, but you've stretched this too far! I quit!

ANNOUNCER: Creepy Terry tiptoes out of the circus. *(Terry exits)*

BOSS: Well, Bobo, that's the end of our list. In a way it's kinda sad to see them all go.

BOBO: But Boss, doesn't this play have a happy ending?

BOSS: Sure Bobo. Everyone will be happy to know that this play is now over.

END

Hot Dog

A MONOLOG

The audience hears only one side of a phone conversation. The only props are a telephone and a shirt or coat that can pass for an ice cream shop uniform.

Hello! This is Richard's Ice Cream Shop...Yes, we had an ad in the paper for dogs for sale...Well, we have some a foot long and some smaller...They came Wednesday. So they've been here about four days...Oh yes, they all came at the same time...What? You thought the larger ones came first?...What color? They're all red...Yes. We can have some ready for Christmas. You want what? One for Judy, one for Jimmy and one for Joey...Whatever you say...What was that about them being broken?...No, lady, the ones that are broken, we don't sell...What do we do to keep the drippings off the floor?...We wrap them in a napkin...Right now they're back here in a box...I guess there are about 50 in a box...Yes, ma'am, it is kinda crowded...Do we have paper under them? Yes, there is paper under each row...No, ma'am, we don't take the papers out until we sell them...What did you say? I should be reported?...45 cents small and 75 cents foot long...Yes, we think that is a good price, too...Registered? No, ma'am, but they have been inspected...Yes, we think that is just as good, too...Look, lady, I'm talking about hot dogs...You don't care about their temperature?...Hair? Lady, our dogs do not have hair on them. Yes, I said no hair...No, they will not grow any later. I told you these...You don't want any sick dogs? You think they are sick because of their high temperature?...Lady! These are hot dogs! Hot dogs! Hot dogs!...Yeah, well same to you! **(hangs up)**

END

ABBOT: That's right, you cannot say anything but two words for the next 10 years. You may go now.

(After Monk Monotony exits, the Sign Carrier crosses the stage carrying the sign that reads TEN YEARS LATER. *Monk Monotony reenters)*

ABBOT: Well, Monk Monotony, your first 10 years are up and you may now say your two words.

MONK MONOTONY: Hard bed.

ABBOT: You may go now.

(As Monk Monotony exits, the Sign Carrier enters with the sign. Monk Monotony reenters)

ABBOT: Well, Monk Monotony, you've served here another 10 years. You may now say your two words.

MONK MONOTONY: Bad food.

ABBOT: You may go now.

(As Monk Monotony exits, the Sign Carrier enters with the sign. Monk Monotony reenters)

ABBOT: Well, Monk Monotony, you've been here yet another 10 years. You may now say your two words.

MONK MONOTONY: I quit. *(he exits)*

ABBOT: *(calling after Monk Monotony)* Well, I'm not surprised. You've been complaining ever since you got here.

SOME DO

This chestnut is still appropriate for a Valentine party or as a lighthearted intro to your talk on sex, love, and dating. *Nancy and Robb Mann*

A guy and a girl are sitting on a park bench.

HE: *(nervously)* Some night.

SHE: Yeah, some night.

HE: Some moon.

SHE: Yeah, some moon.

HE: Some stars.

SHE: Yeah, some stars.

HE: Some park.

SHE: Yeah, some park.

HE: *(moves closer to her, then, using his fingers, notices dew on the bench)* Some dew.

SHE: Well, I don't! *(she slaps him across the face, knocking him off the bench)*

FRONTIER MORTICIAN

Be forewarned—this classic skit with a Western theme is full of puns! It begins on page 18.

CREATIVE THEME SKITS

Put several ordinary objects in as many sacks as you have teams. Objects should be things like: paper clip, Q-Tip, Popsicle stick, etc. Put the same things in each sack and give each team 20 minutes to form a skit around a selected theme. The skit can be serious or funny but each team must use every item in the sack and every team member must be involved.

After the time limit have each team present its skit. *Joe Snow*

FASHION FOLLIES

A crazy fashion show always makes a great skit if it's done with a little creativity. The following ideas work great when you set up the stage for a fashion show, with a good announcer who describes the various fashions, and good "fashion models" (guys or girls) who try to walk and wiggle like real models. The results can really be funny. Use these or think up some of your own.

- **Sack Dress.** A dress made of a potato sack, with more paper sacks hung all over it. Maybe even a sack over the model's head.
- **Dinner Dress.** A dress with menus, napkins, salt and pepper shakers, plates, food, etc., hanging all over it.
- **Spring-Flowered Dress.** Dress with real flowers and springs all over it. Purse can be a bucket with fertilizer, tools, etc.
- **Tea Dress.** A dress with tea bags all over it and a tea pot handbag.
- **Multi-Colored Skirt and Scatter Pin Sweater.** A skirt with crayons and coloring book pictures all over it; the sweater has dozens of safety pins or ball point pens all over it.
- **Buckskin Jacket and Quilted Skirt.** Dollar bills pinned on jacket; a bedspread made into a skirt (quilt) or cotton balls pinned on skirt.
- **Slip-On Sweater with Matched Pants.** A sweater with a slip over it and pants with match books all over.
- **TV Jacket.** A robe with TV guides, antennas, etc., all over it.

Patti Hughes

Frontier Mortician

CHARACTERS
•Announcer •Sam Alamode •Piney "Pie" Alamode
•Trigger Mortis (Trig) •Joe Silver •Arnie

ANNOUNCER: The makers of Fatrical present *(music)* Frontier Mortician...Are you skinny and run down? Are you so thin you have to wear skis in the bathtub to keep from going down the drain? When you turn sideways and stick out your tongue, do you look like a zipper? When you drink strawberry pop, do you look like a thermometer? Then you need Fatrical, the drink that adds weight to you. Fatrical is not a capsule, it is not a solid, it is not a liquid. It's a gas that you inhale. Fatrical comes in one delicious gas flavor— mustard. It costs only $4.95 a case, and the equipment for inhaling it costs only $5,678. This includes a 10,000 cubic foot tank, 300 feet of hose, three pumps, two filter tips, and a partridge in a pear tree. Now for our story—Trigger Mortis, frontier mortician. The scene opens in the residence of Sam Alamode, wealthy rancher and owner of the Bar B Q Ranch in Sparerib, Texas. Sam is dying and is talking to his lovely daughter Piney Alamode, whom he lovingly calls Pie.

SAM: Pie, honey, I'm dying again. Go call Trigger Mortis, the frontier mortician. Have hearse, will travel.

PIE: What's wrong with you, daddy? What's your ailment?

SAM: I swallowed the thermometer and I'm dying by degrees.

PIE: I'll go call Trigger Mortis right now.

ANNOUNCER: Unknown to Sam Alamode, his head foreman, Joe Silver, is hiding outside listening to the conversation.

JOE: Let old Sam die. I wish he would. Then I can take the ranch and be set for life. He's always got some fool disease. Last week he swallowed a dynamite cap and his hair came out in bangs. Before that he swallowed a hydrogen bomb and had atomic ache. He's suffering from flower disease—he's a blooming idiot. Hey, here comes Pie Alamode's stupid boyfriend, Arnie. Poor kid...he's an orphan...little orphan Arnie...I'll just sneak away...

ARNIE: I haven't seen my girlfriend Pie Alamode for two weeks. Boy, she has lovely eyes—one is brown and the other two are blue. Last time she rolled her eyes at me, I picked them up and rolled them back. I remember the first time she kissed me...it made chills go up and down my spine...then I found out her Popsicle was leaking. I'll knock at the door. *(knocks)*

PIE: Who is it?

ARNIE: It's me, honey—and I call you honey cause you have hives.

PIE: Oh, my cookie...and I call you cookie because you're so crummy.

ANNOUNCER: We interrupt this love scene to bring you a message from Peter Pan makeup. Use Peter Pan before your pan peters out. This is the makeup used by the stars—Sylvester Stallone, Sharon Stone, and Beethoven the dog. Listen to this letter from Mrs. Mergatroid Fluglehorn from Liverlip, Mississippi: "My face was so wrinkled I had to screw my hat on. Then I used Peter Pan makeup and I don't look like an old woman anymore—I look like an old man. I had my wrinkles tightened up, and now every time I raise my eyebrows, I pull up my socks. I give all the credit to Peter Pan..." You can be beautiful, too...now back to Frontier Mortician. Trigger Mortis, the frontier mortician, is answering his telephone.

TRIG: Oh, it's you, Miss Pie Alamode. You want me to come to see your father? Well, my hearse has been giving me trouble—I think I blew a casket. I've got to quit using embalming fluid in the gas tank because the motor keeps dying. Yes...yes...well, I have to finish my breakfast. I'm eating Shrouded Wheat and Ghost Toasties...Well, I'll hurry right out. Bye. I must be shoveling off...

ANNOUNCER: Pie Alamode hangs up and goes to meet her lover, little orphan Arnie, in their favorite meeting place—the family graveyard.

PIE: It's so romantic here in the graveyard. There's the grave of my Uncle Earnest. Look, there are some maggots making love in dead earnest.

ARNIE: Darling, may I have your hand in marriage?

PIE: My hand? Oh yes. In fact, you can have my arm, too.

ARNIE: Here, I'll put this ring on your finger.

PIE: Awwww, your face is turning red.

ARNIE: Yeah, and your finger's turning green...after all, we've been going together for 12 years now.

PIE: So what do you want—a pension? Let's go tell my father.

ANNOUNCER: This program is brought to you by the Double Insanity Insurance Company. Mothers, do you have children? Then protect them with a double deal policy. We pay 100 thousand dollars if your son is killed by a herd of white elephants going east on Thursday. If you lose an arm, we help you look for it. If you get hit in the head, we pay you in one lump sum. We have a double indemnity clause, too—if you die in an accident, we bury you twice. Now, a report from the National Safety Council. It is predicted that 356 people will die in accidents this weekend. So far only 135 have been reported. Some of you aren't trying...Now, back to our story. Joe Silver is plotting to kidnap Pie Alamode and hold her for ransom. He thinks Sam Alamode is dying, but he really isn't. Trigger Mortis, frontier mortician, is on his way to the ranch.

TRIG: Well, here I am. When you are at death's door, I will pull you through.

SAM: Good to see you, Trigger. Can you give me a good funeral?

TRIG: I'll give you a good funeral or your mummy back. Could I interest you in our new layaway plan?

SAM: I'm a sick man, a sick man. The doctor told me to drink some medicine after a hot bath, and I can hardly finish drinking the bath.

TRIG: You need some of my Whistler's Mother medicine—one dose and you're off your rocker.

SAM: Trigger, I can trust you, can't I?

TRIG: Of corpse, of corpse. Have I ever let you down?

SAM: I don't trust my head foreman, Joe Silver. He has a sneaky look.

TRIG: I happen to know, Sam, that Joe Silver wants to kidnap your daughter and keep her from marrying little orphan Arnie.

SAM: Trigger, we gotta do something. Think of a plan.

ANNOUNCER: Will Trigger Mortis think of a plan? While he thinks, a word from Honest John Pendergast, the used car dealer. Honest John has bargains in used cars that you can't afford to miss. Here's an 887 Essex. This is a revolutionary car—Washington drove it at Valley Forge. The tires are so beat that you not only knock the pedestrians down, you whip them to death. This program is also brought to you by Glum, the toothpaste that gives your bad breath the Good Housekeeping seal of approval. Are your teeth like the Ten Commandments—all broken? Do you have a Pullman car mouth—one upper and one lower? Then use Glum. Glum contains eucalyptus oil, flown in from Australia. This eucalyptus oil is the secret of Glum. Millions of users say, "Man, you clipt us." Be true to your teeth and they will never be false to you. Now, back to Frontier Mortician. Sam, Pie, Arnie, and Trigger Mortis are trying to figure out how to get rid of Joe Silver.

20

SAM: I have a splitting headache.

TRIG: Have your eyes ever been checked?

SAM: No, they've always been blue. Trigger, why don't we put Joe in one of your coffins and ship him out of the state?

TRIG: A tisket, a tasket, I'll put him in a casket. I was in love once, so I know what Arnie and Pie are going through.

PIE: You were in love?

TRIG: Yes, I was stuck on a girl who worked in the glue factory. She had a schoolgirl complexion...with diplomas under her eyes. Her lips were like petals...bicycle pedals. Those lips...those teeth...that hair...that eye...

ARNIE: Hey, here comes Joe Silver. Get your coffin ready, Trigger.

PIE: Daddy, lie on the bed and act like you're dead.

ANNOUNCER: Sam lies on the bed and holds his breath. Trigger takes off his shoes and everybody holds their breath...At this breathless moment, we bring you the daily police calls. Calling car 15, calling car 15. Happy birthday, car 15, you are now car 16. Car 56, car 56, rush to the Bungling Brother's Circus. The fat woman has hay fever and is crying so much three midgets are about to drown. Car 23, car 23, return the 10-gallon hat bought for the mayor—he has an 11-gallon head. Car 19, go to the corner of sixth and Main—the Chinese cook has just committed chop sueycide...back to the story. Joe Silver enters Sam's bedroom as the other people hide.

JOE: So I finally caught you, you scoundrel. You've cut my check so many times I have to endorse it with Mercurochrome. I want to marry your daughter, Sam, and nobody's gonna stop me. Sure I'm tough...I've been sent up the river so many times I get fan mail from the salmon. The last time they caught me I got 10 years in jail and two in the electric chair. Even when I was a baby people were pinning things on me. Now, I'm gonna get you.

SAM: Get him, Arnie!

TRIG: Quick! I have the casket opened. Push him, Arnie!

JOE: Help! Help! You're pushing me. *(muffled sounds)*

TRIG: That takes care of him. Now I have to run for a body. A fellow in town swallowed a quart of shellac and died. But he had a lovely finish.

ARNIE: How can we thank you? You'll come to the wedding, won't you?

TRIG: Yes, I plan to give you a tombstone for a present, but don't take it for granite.

SAM: Thanks, Trig. By the way, stop over and we'll play golf someday.

TRIG: Don't ever play golf with an undertaker—he's always on top at the last hole.

ARNIE: Now we're alone, Pie, my love. Someday you'll have my name.

PIE: I never did find out—what is your last name, Arnie?

ARNIE: My name is Arnie R. Square.

PIE: What a lovely name I'll have—Mrs. Pie R. Square.

ANNOUNCER: And as the sun sinks slowly in the west, we leave the lovers as they plan their future. Tune in tomorrow for a new adventure, brought to you by Bleeties, the cereal for old goats. Bleeties contains 56% iron, 22% copper, 78% steel, 14% bronze, and 11% zinc. It doesn't snap, crackle, or pop; it lies there and rusts. Bleeties isn't the breakfast of champions—it's for people who just want to get into the semifinals. In closing, be sure to visit your local dime store where they're having a monster sale. Haven't you always wanted to own your own monster? We have vampires at special prices and they're excellent for curing tired blood! These are experienced vampires who worked as tellers in blood banks. Now...tune in tomorrow for the first episode of the new story, "I was a Teen Spinster" brought to you by the gardener's magazine, <u>Weeder's Digest.</u>

END

SMASHING GUITARS

For this skit you need two inexpensive guitars that can be broken up, but are playable. You'll need two singers, one of whom can play the guitar.

This skit works best if the actors are the group leaders or sponsors. Introduce them as a new acoustic group out of Seattle or Nashville or L.A., and give them an appropriate name (Smashing Turnips, Logjam, Floss, etc.)

This kind of slapstick requires some tasteful deadpan acting by both singers. The results are hilarious. Damaged or secondhand guitars sometimes can be obtained inexpensively or for free from some merchants. As the singers begin to sing a folk song, such as "Tom Dooley," have them do the following:

1. BOB begins to sing off-key, annoying **DANI**. **DANI** criticizes **BOB'S** singing and snaps a string on **BOB'S** guitar by pulling hard and letting go.

2. DANI now sings. **BOB** stops her, takes out a pair of wire cutters, and snips all of **DANI'S** strings except one.

3. BOB starts singing again. **DANI** stops him, takes his guitar away, picks up a saw (a big-toothed pruning saw will make short work of the guitar neck!), saws off the neck of **BOB'S** guitar, and hands it back to him.

4. BOB puts what's left of his guitar down, and turns **DANI'S** guitar over. While **DANI** holds the guitar, with the back of the guitar facing the audience, **BOB** sticks a bulls-eye on the back of it, picks up a hammer, aims, and smashes a hole in it.

5. DANI then takes **BOB'S** guitar, puts it on the floor by a chair, gets up on the chair, and gets ready to jump on it. She counts "One! Two! Three!" then jumps. But in the middle of her leap, **BOB** quickly puts **DANI'S** guitar on top of his, with the result that **DANI** smashes both of them.

6. They pick up their guitars, try to put them together as well as possible, finish their song, and leave.

THE ART SHOW

Hang pictures or paintings on a wall at different heights. Have several kids file by the pictures, stopping at each one to look for a moment or to comment to someone about the pictures. All should be dressed in raincoats or overcoats. The final kid comes by inside an overcoat which she holds over

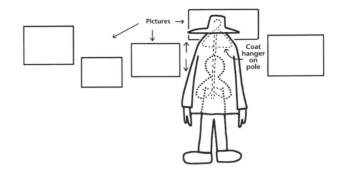

her head on a coat hanger. A hat is placed over the hook of the hanger. As she reaches each picture, she "adjusts her height" by raising or lowering the coat. The effect is really funny. *Bill Chaney*

BELLY WHISTLE

Talk about a throwback to the days of gross camp shenanigans...but oh well. This one is still a crack-up, as long as the setting is as indelicate as the skit.

Announce that you have invited a great new talent to your meeting, Mr. Tummy Tootwhistle, to perform a musical number. Mr. Tootwhistle comes out, which is a guy who has a giant hat covering his head, arms, and shoulders, and has a shirt and bow tie at his waist, with fake arms hanging from his hips. Painted on the guy's bare stomach is a face, with the mouth being his navel, giving the appearance that the mouth is in a "puckered" or whistling position. The guy then whistles a tune, making his stomach go in and out, which looks like puffing cheeks. A tape recording of the whistling can be used if the guy can't whistle very good. This is hysterical to watch and provides a lot of laughs in a meeting.

WHO'S ON FIRST?

This is undeniably one of this century's best and funniest comic routines ever written—or performed, with classic gusto by Abbott and Costello. The only problem with performing this is that it's got to be memorized, not just read. Timing is everything. Try to get a video of Abbott and Costello's rendition of this sketch for your student performers to study. The script begins on page 24.

Who's On First?

CAST

Sports announcer and baseball manager, costumed appropriately

ANNOUNCER: I understand you used to coach a baseball team.

MANAGER: Yes, I did. It was a pretty good team, in fact.

ANNOUNCER: Were your players good enough to make the big leagues?

MANAGER: Well, yes.

ANNOUNCER: Hey, why don't you tell us some of their names, because they might be famous someday.

MANAGER: Okay. Let's see, on the bases we have...Who's on first, What's on second, and I Don't Know is on third.

ANNOUNCER: Wait a minute. You're the manager of the team, aren't you?

MANAGER: Yes.

ANNOUNCER: You're supposed to know all the fellows' names?

MANAGER: Of course.

ANNOUNCER: Okay then, the first baseman's name.

MANAGER: Who.

ANNOUNCER: The guy on first.

MANAGER: Who

ANNOUNCER: The FIRST BASEMAN!

MANAGER: Who is on first base.

ANNOUNCER: I'm asking you who's on first base.

MANAGER: That's the man's name.

ANNOUNCER: That's whose name?

MANAGER: Yes.

ANNOUNCER: Look, all I want to know is, what's the name of the guy on first base?

MANAGER: No, no. What's on second.

ANNOUNCER: Who's on second?

MANAGER: Who's on first.

ANNOUNCER: I don't know.

MANAGER: He's on third.

ANNOUNCER: Third base? Look, how'd we get on third base?

MANAGER: Well, you mentioned the man's name.

ANNOUNCER: Who's name?

MANAGER: No, Who is on first.

ANNOUNCER: I don't know.

MANAGER: He's on third.

ANNOUNCER: Hey, if I mentioned the guy's name, who did I say was on third?

MANAGER: Who is on first.

ANNOUNCER: I'm not asking you who's on first—

MANAGER: Who is on first.

ANNOUNCER: I want to know what's the name of the guy on third base.

MANAGER: No, What's on second.

ANNOUNCER: Who's on second?

MANAGER: Who's on first.

ANNOUNCER: I DON'T KNOW!

MANAGER: Third base.

ANNOUNCER: All right. Just forget the infield. Let's go to the outfield. Do you have a left fielder?

MANAGER: Of course we have a left fielder.

ANNOUNCER: The left fielder's name?

MANAGER: Why.

ANNOUNCER: Well, I just thought I'd ask.

MANAGER: Well, I just thought I'd tell you.

ANNOUNCER: Then go ahead and tell me: What's the left fielder's name?

MANAGER: What's on second.

ANNOUNCER: Who's on second?

MANAGER: Who's on first.

ANNOUNCER: I DON'T KNOW!

BOTH: Third base.

ANNOUNCER: Let's try again. The left fielder's name?

MANAGER: Why.

ANNOUNCER: Because.

MANAGER: Oh, he's our center fielder.

ANNOUNCER: *(exasperated)* Look, let's go back to the infield. Do you pay your guys anything?

MANAGER: As a matter of fact, yes. We give them a little something for uniforms, et cetera.

ANNOUNCER: Okay. Look, it's payday and all the guys are lined up to get paid. The first baseman is standing at the front of the line. Now he reaches out to you to accept his money. Now, who gets the money?

MANAGER: That's right.

ANNOUNCER: So who gets the money?

MANAGER: Yes, of course. Why not? He's entitled to it.

ANNOUNCER: Who is?

MANAGER: Certainly. Why, sometimes even his mother takes the money for him.

ANNOUNCER: Whose mother?

MANAGER: Yes.

ANNOUNCER: Look, all I'm trying to find out is what's the name of your first baseman.

MANAGER: What's on second.

ANNOUNCER: Who's on second?

MANAGER: Who's on first.

ANNOUNCER: I don't know.

MANAGER: Third base.

ANNOUNCER: Okay, okay. I'll try again. Do you have a pitcher?

MANAGER: Of course we have a pitcher. What kind of team would we be without a pitcher?

ANNOUNCER: The pitcher's name?

MANAGER: Tomorrow.

ANNOUNCER: What time?

MANAGER: What time what?

ANNOUNCER: What time tomorrow are you gonna tell me who's pitching?

MANAGER: How many times do I have to tell you? Who is on first.

ANNOUNCER: You say "Who's on first" one more time and I'll break your arm. I want to know what's your pitcher's name?

MANAGER: What's on second.

ANNOUNCER: Who's on second?

MANAGER: Who's on first.

ANNOUNCER: I don't know.

MANAGER: He's on third.

ANNOUNCER: The catcher's name?

MANAGER: Today.

ANNOUNCER: Today. Tomorrow. What kind of team is this? All right. Let me set up a hypothetical play. Now, Tomorrow's pitching. Today's catching. I am up at bat. Tomorrow pitches to me and I bunt the ball down the first base line. Today being the good catcher that he is, runs down the first base line, picks up the ball, and throws it to the first baseman. Now, when he throws the ball to the first baseman, who gets the ball?

MANAGER: That's the first right thing you've said all night.

ANNOUNCER: I don't even know what I'm talking about. Look, if he throws the ball to first, somebody has to catch it. So who gets the ball?

MANAGER: Naturally.

ANNOUNCER: Who catches it?

MANAGER: Naturally.

ANNOUNCER: Ohhhhhh. Today picks up the ball and throws it to Naturally.

MANAGER: He does nothing of the kind. He throws the ball to Who.

ANNOUNCER: Naturally.

MANAGER: Right.

ANNOUNCER: I just said that. You say it.

MANAGER: He picks up the ball and throws it to Who.

ANNOUNCER: Naturally.

MANAGER: That's what I'm saying.

ANNOUNCER: Look. Bases are loaded. Somebody gets up to bat and hits a line drive to Who. Who throws to What. What throws to I Don't Know. Triple play! Next batter gets up and hits a long ball to Why. Because? I Don't Know! He's on third and I just don't give a darn!

MANAGER: What?

ANNOUNCER: I said I don't give a darn!

MANAGER: Hey, he's our shortstop!

END

THE GOBBLEWART

This is a goofy camp skit, but funny if it's hammed up enough by the actors.

The scene takes place in a pet shop where the proprietor is standing behind a counter. A customer enters the shop and inquires about pets, especially of a dog about three years old and housebroken. The proprietor answers that he is all out of dogs, but she may be interested in a "gobblewart."

As she wonders what in the world that is, he points to a "blob" on the floor (a person hunched over on the floor). She exclaims that it certainly is ugly, but what does it do? He states that it can be very handy around the house for it will eat anything.

Immediately a girl comes running into the room screaming, "The gorilla is loose!" The gorilla (played by another person) comes lumbering into the room, but the proprietor calmly says, "Gobblewart, the gorilla." With this the gobblewart pounces upon and kills the gorilla.

The girl returns running into the room, shouting, "The lion's loose, the lion's loose!" The lion comes into the room and the proprietor calmly states, "Gobblewart, the lion." The gobblewart pounces on the lion and kills it.

The customer is amazed and states that that is wonderful and that she'll take it.

The next scene takes place at the customer's home. A friend (or spouse) enters the room and asks if she got the dog she wanted. She tells him of the gobblewart and points to the blob on the floor. He laughs and laughs and then exclaims, "Gobblewart, my foot." With this the gobblewart attacks his foot as he runs off stage.

TUG-OF-WAR SKIT

You need a room with two separate doorways up toward the front—or a room divider that blocks the view of the audience. The skit should take place while someone else is talking—giving announcements, explaining the retreat schedule—so that the skit distracts audience.

A boy comes out of one of the doors, tugging for all he's worth on a heavy rope. He struggles with this while pulling it across the stage and out the other door. A second or two later, as soon as he's disappeared from sight, and while the rope is still moving across the stage, he reappears in the first door on the other end of the same rope,

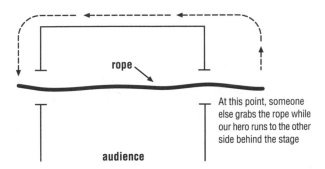

rope

audience

At this point, someone else grabs the rope while our hero runs to the other side behind the stage

except this time he's pulling vainly against the tugging as he is now *dragged* across the stage and out the second door. *Pete Steveson*

PING-PONG SKIT

Find two people who can make loud "clicks" in the roof of their mouths with their tongues, a sound like a Ping-Pong ball hitting a paddle.

They each hold a paddle and begin playing on an imaginary table, making the sound effects with their mouths. They gradually get farther and farther apart, making the "clicks" farther apart, too.

Finally, they get so far apart, they disappear offstage (or exit outside doors). When they reappear, they have switched positions and are walking in backward, continuing their game; but now it looks like they are hitting the ball all the way around the world. They continue playing and walking backward toward each other until they bump into each other, turn around, and start a fast game facing each other as before. *David Coppedge*

THE MONA LISA

Have someone memorize the words to the old Nat King Cole song "Mona Lisa." Then dress someone up as Leonardo d'Vinci's Mona Lisa herself—black wig, black robe, and black shawl. Build a picture frame out of old boards and have Mona sit behind it, with that enigmatic half smile on her face. Drape a sheet from the bottom of the picture frame to the floor so that the audience cannot see the Mona Lisa's feet.

As the song begins, the curtain opens to reveal the Mona Lisa. The singer turns toward the Mona Lisa and sings to the picture. However, whenever the singer turns his back to the picture, Mona acts

out of character; she picks her nose, sneezes, cleans out her ear, shoots water at the singer from a water gun, blows a kiss to the singer, eats a banana, and does other crazy stunts. Finally Mona hits the singer in the face with a whipped cream pie, at which point the singer jumps into the picture frame and chases the Mona Lisa. *E. Paul Albrecht and Roy J. Delozier*

SUMO WRESTLERS

For this skit you will need two guys, preferably of a muscular or flabby physique, dressed in diapers (use a white sheet for the diapers). You will also need an announcer with a good voice and a simulated (or real) microphone.

The two wrestlers stomp into the room, circle each other, and snort. The announcer introduces the first wrestler as Yamahaha, who then steps forward, bows with folded hands, and slowly laughs, with a deep voice and a Japanese accent, "Ha ha

ha ha ha!" He then throws rice over each shoulder. This procedure is repeated when the announcer introduces Korimot-ho, who responds with a "Ho ho ho ho."

After their introductions the two wrestlers fight. They are never to touch each other or to speak, except for occasional "Ha ha's" and "Ho ho's." Each fighter does to himself what he really wants to do to his opponent. The opponent responds—at the same time—by reacting to whatever hold or punch as if it had really been directed at him.

While this is going on, the announcer calls the play-by-play describing finger bends, nostril lifts, toe stomps, navel jabs, armpit hair pulls, etc. With good actors, this event is hilarious. *Bob and Doug McKenzie*

COUNTRY EAR WASH

This skit needs five people—a narrator and four helpers who need to be prepped beforehand. The narrator introduces it this way:

> I recently visited my great aunt who lived most of her life in the old country, and she told me about the strangest custom that I had a chance to actually participate in. She called it the Country Ear Wash. It's so interesting that I'd like to demonstrate it for you—and for that I've brought with me four descendants of Old World families.
>
> What I have here is an old glass jar with fresh spring water. The water must be very pure. And now, the Country Ear Wash.

At this point the narrator takes a swig from the jar and pretends to slosh the water around inside his head, as if he were washing out his ears from the inside. After a minute or two of this, he motions the second person in the line to bend down, then pretends to spit the water into his ear.

And so on. While this is going on, a little ad-libbing goes a long way—the four who aren't washing their ears can banter about how long it's been since their ears have had a good cleaning, about how much better they can hear now that they've had a good old country ear wash, etc.

The fifth and last person in line follows suit with the ear-washing routine—but all the time he's been holding a mouthful of chocolate syrup. So when he's done cleaning his ears and spits the "water" out, the audience sees only thick brown gunk dribbling down his chin. *Teen Valley Ranch*

MAGIC BANDANA

A messy, hilarious skit—perfect for any occasion you need hypercomic relief (page 30).

TARZAN

This Oxford-educated Tarzan makes for a fun parody of the ol' Johnny Weissmuller hero (page 31). *Tom McKee*

SURREAL MASHED POTATOES

This is true performance art—the pseudo-existential skit. The point of it is that there is no point—though with good acting, the audience is convinced there is a point, but they're just missing it.

There's very little script, and what there is can be ad-libbed.

A man comes into a restaurant (table and chair) and sits down. Waitress comes in and asks for order.

MAN: I'll have a big pot of mashed potatoes.

WAITRESS: Is that all?

MAN: Yup.

WAITRESS: No beverage?

MAN: Nope. Just a big pot of mashed potatoes.

WAITRESS: No salad or soup or dessert or anything?

MAN: Listen! All I want is a big pot of mashed potatoes.

WAITRESS: Well, okay. I'll tell the cook. *(Waitress goes back into a wing offstage and in a voice which everyone can hear, tells the cook that there's a weirdo out there who wants a big pot of mashed potatoes)*

COOK: Is that all?

WAITRESS: Yup. That's all he wants.

COOK: No salad?

WAITRESS: Nope.

COOK: No beverage or anything?

WAITRESS: Nope, just a big pot of mashed potatoes.

(Argument goes on for a while. Finally the cook relents and gives the waitress a huge pot of mashed potatoes. Use the biggest pot you can. Waitress brings the pot of potatoes out to the customer. He looks around suspiciously, lowers pot to floor, and sticks his head as far into the potatoes as he can—up to his neck. Then he proceeds to jam them into his mouth, his ears, pockets, down his shirt, etc. The waitress, standing there and watching all this, finally asks the man—)

WAITRESS: What the heck are you doing with all those mashed potatoes, anyway?

MAN: *(slowly looks up at waitress with question mark on his face)* Mashed potatoes? I thought this was spinach! *(stands up, turns, and walks out.)*

WAITRESS: *(looks confused for a moment, looks at the pot of mashed potatoes, then suddenly understands)* Spinach…oh, I get it. *(and she dives into the pot of potatoes head first, mushing them all over the place, in her hair, her mouth, etc. Meanwhile, the cook appears, stops, looks shocked, and watches the waitress's potatoe pandemonium from the side of the stage. Finally she gets up and leaves.)*

COOK: *(the light comes on for the cook, who yells—)* Spinach! Yes, spinach! I get it! Oh, boy, is that ever funny! *(and he hits the pot of potatoes like the man and the waitress)*

With any luck, now everyone in the audience is thoroughly confused. At this point someone walks across the stage with a sign that says WHAT IS "SPINACH" SPELLED BACKWARD? Someone you've planted in the audience then jumps up, yelling that, oh, now he gets it—and he dives into the pot, mushing it all over himself.

End the skit with the announcer coming out and suggesting to the crowd that if they think about it for a while, they'll get it. Or she can apologize to the audience for such a lousy skit—until, in midsentence, she pauses, reflects a moment, then says something like, "Spinach spelled backward…spinach spelled backwards…ooohhh, I get it now." And into the pot the announcer goes. *John Splinter*

CHARACTERS
•Magician (dressed in tails, top hat, etc.) •Herkimer, the assistant (appears to be a klutz; never speaks, like Harpo Marx)

PROPS
•Table with a red bandana or handkerchief on top •Banana in a sack

· ·

MAGICIAN: Ladies and gentlemen, today I am going to perform for you my famous vanishing bandana trick. My assistant, Herkimer, will go to the table behind me, and do exactly as I say. And even though I will not look at Herkimer or the bandana, I will be able to make it disappear in Herkimer's hand. *(to Herkimer)* All right, Herkimer...go to the table behind me. *(Herkimer goes to the table. The Magician stands in front, facing the audience, so that he cannot see the table or Herkimer. Make sure the audience can see Herkimer)*

MAGICIAN: Herkimer, please pick up the bandana. *(Herkimer looks at the bandana, but is distracted by the sack lunch under the table, so he picks it up and looks inside the bag. He discovers a banana. Then he looks puzzled, as if he's not sure exactly what the Magician asked him to pick up, so he throws the bandana on the floor, and holds the banana instead)*

MAGICIAN: Herkimer, take the bandana in your right hand, please. *(Herkimer holds the banana in his right hand)*

MAGICIAN: Now, Herkimer, fold the four corners of the bandana together. *(Herkimer begins peeling the banana, counting one, two, three, four. Then he throws the peel on the floor)*

MAGICIAN: Now, Herkimer, fold the bandana in half. *(Herkimer folds the banana in half)*

MAGICIAN: Now stuff the bandana into your left fist and don't let any of it show, Herkimer. *(Herkimer takes the banana and crams it into his fist; the banana oozes out from between his fingers)*

MAGICIAN: Finally, Herkimer, on the count of three, throw the bandana up into the air, and the bandana will be gone! One...two...three. *(On the count of three, Herkimer throws the mashed banana at the Magician and the Magician chases Herkimer off the stage)*

END

TARZAN

CHARACTERS

•Tarzan (dressed in something resembling a loincloth or leopard skin) •Colonel Grub, the villain (in safari getup—at least a pith helmet) •Chief (in African native garb) •Jive (Tarzan's young sidekick) •Oolababe (the chief's daughter) •Narrator

PROPS

•Rope set up to swing across stage, if possible •Long rubber snake •Cap gun •Rubber knife

In the jungle Jive is tied to a pole with wood around, ready to be burned at the stake.

NARRATOR: Darkest Africa! Wild and fore-boding! Man-killing beasts stalk their prey in these dark jungles, ready at any moment to spring, and proceed to tear and mangle. Wild savages lurk in dense underbrush waiting to inflict death upon unwary travelers. So sit right back and relax, as we present "Tarzan."

COLONEL: Hi there! I'm the villain tonight! So far, I've burned down the village of the Lumbago tribe, I've captured Tarzan's little friend Jive—and worst of all, I've said nasty things to the animals! But still, Tarzan hasn't shown up!

TARZAN: *(Tarzan enters, swinging on a rope, and yelling)* AHH... EEEEE... AHHH... EEEEE... AHHH... WAAYA!

COLONEL: Oh-oh! That's Tarzan now! *(to Tarzan)* Me Colonel Grub! You Tarzan! Tarzan want boy to live? Tarzan listen to me! Me boss! You slave! Savvy?

TARZAN: Tell me, Colonel, have you had this speech problem all your life?

COLONEL: Why, why y-you speak as good as me!

TARZAN: Wrong again, Colonel! You mean "as well as I!" And no, I happen to speak <u>better</u> than you do.

COLONEL: B-But when did all this happen? What happened to your English?

TARZAN: Well, Jane isn't with me any longer, so I spend my evenings brushing up on my English.

COLONEL: I couldn't care less! Good English or bad English, the situation remains the same: either you take orders from me or the boy dies!

TARZAN: Big deal—I hardly know the kid. *(Chief enters)*

CHIEF: Ungowah! Tarzan in big trouble! Tarzan burn down village of Lumbagos!

TARZAN: I didn't burn down your village!

CHIEF: We put Tarzan in cobra pit. If Tarzan speak truth, cobra will not kill!

TARZAN: Cobra pit? Isn't it enough if I say, "Cross my heart and hope to die?"

COLONEL: What are you afraid of, Tarzan? I've heard that you're the friend of a million jungle animals.

TARZAN: I am. Unfortunately, there are a million and a half in this jungle! Besides, it was probably you who burned this village.

COLONEL: Perhaps…but how will you prove it?

TARZAN: With my knowledge of the jungle, it would be easy to follow footprints, search for matches and gasoline in your tent, sift through ashes—

COLONEL: Resorting to evidence, eh? The oldest trick in the book! But it won't work among these savages. They believe in the judgment of the cobra. So into the pit!

TARZAN: What are you going to do with the boy?

CHIEF: He stay tied up! Any friend of Tarzan's no friend of ours!

TARZAN: That's unfair! Why not put the kid in with the cobra and tie me up to the tree?

JIVE: Tarzan! How can you talk like that! I've been at your side every waking moment for the past nine years!

TARZAN: Which is precisely why I'm talking like this.

CHIEF: Enough! Into the pit! *(Tarzan exits)*

NARRATOR: Once in the pit, our fearless hero gains the friendship of the cobra— once again proving that all jungle animals love Tarzan. *(Tarzan enters with snake over shoulder)*

CHIEF: Ancient tribal code say, "Since Tarzan make friend with cobra, Tarzan must be telling truth."

COLONEL: Hold on, Chief. I wanted Tarzan to help me trap elephants for ivory. But I don't need him—your tribe can help me instead! Follow my orders and I'll make you rich!

CHIEF: However, <u>modern</u> tribal code say: "Since you offer us a good deal, ancient tribal code don't stand a chance!" We follow!

TARZAN: Don't do it, Chief! Don't you see this man's intentions are dubious, insidious, and furtive?

COLONEL: And my first order as your leader is to kill the loinclothed Noah Webster!

TARZAN: Stop! After years of companionship and understanding, you can't kill me like that! You aren't that savage!

CHIEF: Right! We must repay him for his kindness! Count to five, *then* kill!

NARRATOR: Tarzan, realizing that he is doomed, proceeds to bellow out one of his famous ear-splitting jungle cries—which momentarily deafens those around him, enabling him to flee to freedom among the familiar jungle surroundings. *(Tarzan flees)*

TARZAN: Now to see what Colonel Grub is up to! Holy anthills! They're going to burn Jive at the stake! If I didn't have laundry to do, I'd surely go to his aid…wait a minute! Jive does my laundry! Darn! Now I've got to save him! Okay, Colonel! Drop the gun!

CHIEF: Okay, Tarzan! Drop the knife!

COLONEL: You'll be sorry you came back, Tarzan! Okay Chief! Run him through, then—

TARZAN: Wait, Chief! I appeal to you!

CHIEF: Sorry! Tarzan do not appeal to me! Not even in that miniskirt!

OOLABABE: Wait! Stop! Spare Tarzan's life! Kill me instead!

TARZAN: Oolababe! You're the Chief's daughter! Why do you want to save my life?!

OOLABABE: Because Tarzan teach me how to love and kiss and—

TARZAN: Oolababe, stop! Don't say another word!

OOLABABE: Oolababe's big heart say Tarzan must live!

TARZAN: Yeah...but Oolababe's big <u>mouth</u> say Tarzan must die.

CHIEF: Enough fooling around! We settle this mess with big fight to finish! If Tarzan loses and is killed, then he must be put to death!

TARZAN: You're being a trifle redundant, Chief. Grammatically, the proper phrasing would be—

CHIEF: Hold your filthy tongue in front of maiden! Have you no respect for an innocent girl? The iron tooth will show the truth!

TARZAN: You mean that knife will decide on life?

COLONEL: Enough dumb rhyme! You're wasting time! *(Oolababe shoots the Colonel)*

OOLABABE: The job is done! I used the gun!

CHIEF: One more poem and I go home!

TARZAN: Oolababe! How could you kill him like that?

OOLABABE: I knew you couldn't! You're too chicken! Besides, after you spare him, he turn around and stab you in the back!!

CHIEF: Oolababe speak the truth! I was blinded by promises of wealth! But now Colonel Grub is dead and Tarzan lives! Tarzan do another show next week! And week after that! And summer reruns! Chief no fool! He know which side of bread to butter up! *(Chief exits)*

JIVE: Tarzan, I'm free! They set me free!

TARZAN: Oh, yeah…well, I can always console myself with the fact that there will always be other villains willing to kill a kid!

JIVE: What can I do to repay you for saving my life?

TARZAN: Just a simple token of appreciation will be enough. Like a whalebone slingshot.

JIVE: But the nearest whales are in the Arctic, a jillion miles from here!

TARZAN: Dress warmly, kid. As for you, Oolababe...I think we should continue your lessons. *(Tarzan and Oolababe exit)*

END

MUNCHKIN SKIT

This classic stunt requires two people who are reasonably creative. It works best when presented on a stage with a curtain and only a spotlight for light.

Props you'll need:

• Table covered with a sheet or blanket
• Man's long-sleeved shirt
• Bermuda shorts
• Shoes (large work shoes are best)
• Paper bag containing one toothbrush, a can of shaving cream, a safety razor (without the blade), a banana, a peanut butter-and-jelly sandwich, a cream pie
• Towel, placed on the table

The lead person in this skit should be someone who can ad-lib reasonably well. He stands behind the table with his hands in the shoes. A helper stands directly behind him and puts his hands through the sleeves of the shirt. The shorts go around the lead man's arms.

During the course of the skit it will be necessary for the "munchkin" to shave, brush his teeth, eat, etc. The arms will be doing all the activity and of course the arms can't see what they're doing. The movement should be exaggerated by smearing toothpaste all over the lead man's nose, brushing his cheeks, sticking a banana in his eye, etc. The feet can also do some funny things by clicking heels together, running, etc.

The lead man's monologue can be hilarious. One good idea is to have the munchkin hitch-hiking to some event (that you want to advertise). Explain to the audience that you are going to a certain place and need a ride. Several cars go by. Finally, one stops and the munchkin gets in (although he does not actually move anywhere). He talks to the driver of the car and explains where he is going and asks if he can shave before he gets there. He does and then asks if he can eat his lunch. After he eats his lunch, he brushes his teeth, gets out of the car, and thanks the driver. If the munchkin is a girl, change the costume to a woman's wardrobe and supply beauty aids, such as lipstick, mascara, etc. Then have a beauty class. The more creative and uninhibited the participants are, the more successful the skit will be.

RINSE THE BLOOD OFF MY TOGA

With apologies to William Shakespeare, we give you, starting on page 35, the classic, witty parody of the bard's *Julius Caesar*, though in the fashion of "Dragnet," that mother of all detective shows ("Just the facts, ma'am"). Or you can give it a Brooklyn gumshoe twist. Perform it readers-theater style, with scripts in hand—or memorized, costumed, and with props. In either case, you'll want to rehearse it at least once or twice, depending on the talent of your actors.

FRACTURED FINGER

You will need a pair of gloves and a small, firm carrot. Without the kids seeing you, put a small carrot inside the middle finger of the left glove (see figure 1). Fold back the middle finger on your left hand against your palm and then put the glove on (figure 2). Keep all the fingers of your gloved hand together so that the carrot finger looks like a real finger. With both gloves on, show the kids the back of your gloved hands (figure 3). Hold the carrot finger firmly by pressing on it with the thumb of the same hand (figure 4). With your right hand, grip the carrot finger and quickly break the carrot, yelling and screaming. The kids will think you really broke your finger (figure 5). *Les Christie*

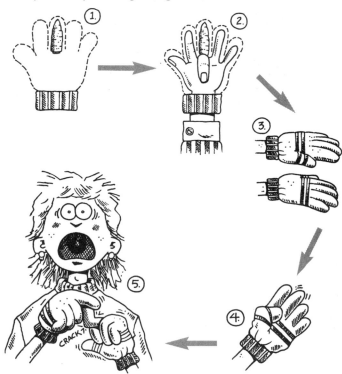

RINSE THE BLOOD OFF MY TOGA

CHARACTERS

•Flavius Maximus •Secretary •Brutus •Calpurnia •Senators (three or four will do) •Mark Antony •Claudius •Tiberius •Sergeant

PROPS

(some of these are optional, depending on how elaborate a performance you want)

•Bag of coins (play or real) •Second bag (weighted as if full of something—ears, in this case) •Onion impaled on a spear
•A dozen play daggers •A table or counter top (for the scene at Claudius's Bar & Grill) •Megaphone

---

The scene: Rome, 44 B.C.

FLAVIUS: *(to audience)* My name is Flavius Maximus. I'm a private Roman eye. My license number is IXIVLLCCDIXM. Also comes in handy as an eye chart. Tonight, I'm going to tell you about the Julius Caesar caper. It all began during the Ides of March. I was in my office. I'd just sent another criminal to jail...Sutonius, the Gladiator. He'd been fixing fights at the Coliseum. Had a crooked lion that kept taking a dive. Anyway, as I was sitting there, my secretary walked in.

SECRETARY: Good morning, Flavius. Here's the mail.

FLAVIUS: Easy with those marble postcards. Break my table. Anything else, babe?

SECRETARY: Yeah. There's somebody outside to see you. Seems awfully excited about something.

FLAVIUS: Show him in, doll.

SECRETARY: Would you come in, sir?

BRUTUS: Thank you, miss. You Flavius Maximus, private Roman eye?

FLAVIUS: Yeh, what's on your mind?

BRUTUS: Are you positive we're alone?

FLAVIUS: I'm positive we're alone.

BRUTUS: Well, who's that standing beside you?

FLAVIUS: That's you, stupid. *(to audience)* I could see l was dealing with no ordinary man. This guy was a nut! *(to Brutus)* Okay, what's on your mind?

BRUTUS: Flavius Maximus, a terrible thing has happened. It's the greatest crime in the history of Rome.

FLAVIUS: Awright, give it to me straight. What's up?

BRUTUS: Julius Caesar has been murdered!

FLAVIUS: Julius Caesar murdered! *(to audience)* I couldn't believe my ears! Big Juli was dead!

BRUTUS: Yeh, he was killed just 20 minutes ago. It happened in the Senate. He was stabbed.

FLAVIUS: Stabbed?

BRUTUS: Yeh, They got him right in the rotunda!

FLAVIUS: Oh, that's a painful spot. I had a splinter there once.

BRUTUS: Yeh.

FLAVIUS: Those marble splinters, you know.

BRUTUS: Boy, I tell you, all of Rome is in an uproar. I came to you because you're the top private eye in Rome. You've got to find the killer.

FLAVIUS: Well, I'll try.

BRUTUS: Aw, you can do it. After all, you're the guy who got Nero. You sent him up on that arson rap.

FLAVIUS: Oh yeah, Nero. The whole town was sure burnt up about him, eh? Ha, ha. Get it? The whole town. Shades of Jupiter!

BRUTUS: Well, look. What do you say Flavius? Will you take the case?

FLAVIUS: Just a minute, pal. I like to know who I'm working for. Just who are you?

BRUTUS: I'm a senator. I was Caesar's best friend. The name's Brutus.

FLAVIUS: Brutus, eh? Okay, Brutus, you got yourself a boy. I'll take the case. My fee is 125 drachmas a day—payable in advance.

BRUTUS: Okay, here you are. *(sound of money)*

FLAVIUS: You're one short.

BRUTUS: Hey, you got a good ear.

FLAVIUS: When it comes to money, perfect pitch. Let's go, eh? *(to audience)* We went outside, flagged a passing chariot, and made our way down the Via Apia. The streets were crowded with the usual people—slaves, legionnaires, patricians, and little men who came out of doorways and sold you postcards from Gaul. Before long we found ourselves at the Senate. *(sounds of men in Senate)*

BRUTUS: Well, Flavius, this is where it happened. This is where Big Juli got knocked off.

FLAVIUS: So where's the corpus delicti?

BRUTUS: The what?

FLAVIUS: The corpus delicti. What's a matter, don't you understand plain Latin? The body!

BRUTUS: Oh, the stiff.

FLAVIUS: Yeah.

BRUTUS: Oh, he's laying right over there.

FLAVIUS: Wowee! Eight daggers in him.

BRUTUS: Yeh, what do you think?

FLAVIUS: If he were alive today, he'd be a pretty sick boy!

BRUTUS: Yeh.

FLAVIUS: He's really fixed for blades, eh? Ha, ha.

BRUTUS: Aw, come on, Flavius. You gotta solve this crime.

FLAVIUS: Okay, okay. Fill me in. Who are those guys over there?

BRUTUS: They were all here when it happened. That's Publius…that's Casca…there's Tribonius.

FLAVIUS: I see. Who's that guy over there with the lean-and-hungry look on his kisser?

BRUTUS: That's Cassius.

FLAVIUS: Yeh, looks like a loser from the Coliseum. Now, who do you think is the likeliest suspect?

BRUTUS: That fellow next to him.

FLAVIUS: Wait a minute, that's you.

BRUTUS: I know, but can I be trusted?

FLAVIUS: *(to audience)* I could see I was dealing with no ordinary case. This was a mental case. *(sound of walking)* Wait a minute. Who's the dame?

BRUTUS: That's Caesar's wife. Her name is Calpurnia.

FLAVIUS: Yeh, well, she's a suspect.

BRUTUS: Sure.

FLAVIUS: Pardon me, Mrs. Caesar?

CALPURNIA: Yes?

FLAVIUS: Flavius Maximus, private Roman eye. I'd like to ask you a few questions. What do you know about this?

CALPURNIA: I told him. I told him, "Juli, don't go."

FLAVIUS: What?

CALPURNIA: "Juli, don't go," I told him. No, he wouldn't listen to me.

FLAVIUS: Now look, Mrs. Caesar, I—

CALPURNIA: If I told him once, I told him a thousand times, "Juli, don't go..."

FLAVIUS: Now, please don't upset yourself...

CALPURNIA: I begged him, don't go. I told him, "Juli, don't go." I said, "It's the Ides of March. Beware, already."

FLAVIUS: Yeah, but—

CALPURNIA: But would he listen to his wife? No!

FLAVIUS: Take it easy! Sergeant, take Mrs. Caesar home.

SERGEANT: Come along, ma'am. Come along.

CALPURNIA: I told him, "Juli, don't go." *(fade out)* I told him, "Juli, don't go," but would he listen to me? No. But I warned him, "Juli, don't go…"

FLAVIUS: I don't blame him for going! All right, you senators. You can go, too, but don't leave town. *(senators mumble)*

BRUTUS: Well, what do you think?

FLAVIUS: I don't know! Not an angle anywhere. Not a clue.

BRUTUS: Well, cheer up, Flavius. After all, Rome wasn't built in a day.

FLAVIUS: What was that?

BRUTUS: I said, Rome wasn't built in a day.

FLAVIUS: That's very good—Rome wasn't built in a day—very good.

BRUTUS: You like it?

FLAVIUS: Yeah.

BRUTUS: It's yours.

FLAVIUS: Thanks. Let's reconstruct the crime. Now, Caesar was over there and—

BRUTUS: Right over here, yeah.

FLAVIUS: Shh!

BRUTUS: What's the matter?

FLAVIUS: Somebody is behind that pillar. I'll go get him. Hush. *(pause)* Okay buddy. Come on. Come on out. What are you doing here?

MARK: *(cries out in agony)* Stop it.

FLAVIUS: What are you doin' hangin' around here, buster?

MARK: Why shouldn't I? I'm Mark Antony.

FLAVIUS: Mark Antony?

MARK: Yeh, l just made a speech over the body of Caesar. I said, "Friends, Romans, countrymen, lend me your ears!"

FLAVIUS: Yeah? What you got in that sack?

MARK: Ears.

FLAVIUS: Get outta here!

MARK: Wait a minute. Don't you want to know who bumped off Julius Caesar?

FLAVIUS: You know who did it? Out with it. What's his name?

MARK: His name is—ahh oooooo eeeee ohhhhh ahhhhh.

FLAVIUS: That's a funny name. Must be Greek.

BRUTUS: No, look! He's dead.

FLAVIUS: *(to audience)* What a confusing case. All I got for clues is two dead bodies and a sackful of ears.

BRUTUS: Now, look, Flavius. I'm paying you 100 drachmas a day.

FLAVIUS: 125 drachmas.

BRUTUS: That's right. You got a good ear.

FLAVIUS: I got a sackful of good ears.

BRUTUS: Let's have some action here.

FLAVIUS: Don't get your toga in a knot. Listen, I got a pal. Claudius. Runs a bar on the Via Flaminia. He should have a few answers for me.

BRUTUS: That's the idea. Get out among the people, ask questions. After all, when in Rome, do as the Romans do.

FLAVIUS: What was that one? What was that one?

BRUTUS: I said, when in Rome, do as the Romans do.

FLAVIUS: That's very good—when in Rome, do as the Romans do.

BRUTUS: You like it?

FLAVIUS: Yeah.

BRUTUS: It's yours.

FLAVIUS: Thanks. I'll see you later.

BRUTUS: See ya!

FLAVIUS: *(to the audience)* Claudius's Bar & Grill is a hangout where I get all the answers. It's just a small place with a few tables and a guy in the corner playing a reed pipe.

CLAUDIUS: Hi ya, Flav.

FLAVIUS: Hi, Claud. What's new?

CLAUDIUS: Nothing much. Whatcha drinkin'?

FLAVIUS: Give me a martinus.

CLAUDIUS: You mean a martini.

FLAVIUS: If I want two, I'll ask for 'em. Look, I'm working on this Julius Caesar kill. You know anything?

CLAUDIUS: Try that dame over there. *(her back is to Flavius)*

FLAVIUS: Okay sister, start talkin'.

CALPURNIA: *(she turns around, and guess who...)* I told him, "Juli, don't go!"

FLAVIUS: Oh, no!

CALPURNIA: Juli, don't go...

FLAVIUS: Out! Out!

CLAUDIUS: Hey, Flavius. I think I know the guy you're looking for.

FLAVIUS: You mean...Mr. Big?

CLAUDIUS: Yeah. His name is—ooooooo eeeeeee aaaaaaaa eeeeeeeeeeeg.

FLAVIUS: Now that's an interesting name. I'd like to write that down—got a chisel? Claudius? Claudius! *(to audience)* I'd never get any more conversation from him. He was dead. This was shaping up bigger than I thought. Suddenly l looked up. There was Brutus.

BRUTUS: Hello, Flavius.

FLAVIUS: Brutus, what are you doing here?

BRUTUS: Hey, I was lookin' for ya. Who's that there on the floor?

FLAVIUS: Claudius, the bartender.

BRUTUS: Hey, that's a funny place for him to carry a knife—in his back.

FLAVIUS: He's dead. He was stabbed through the portico.

BRUTUS: That's even more painful than the rotunda.

FLAVIUS: Yeah.

BRUTUS: Have you come up with any answers? Who killed Julius Caesar?

FLAVIUS: *(to audience)* I started to think and slowly the pieces fell into place. Brutus was the only man around when all those guys got killed—Caesar, Anthony, the bartender—Brutus was always there. Things were beginning to add up. I put two and two together and it came out IV. It was time to make my move.

BRUTUS: What do you mean, IV?

FLAVIUS: Four, stupid.

BRUTUS: Well, have you come up with any answers? Who killed Julius Caesar?

FLAVIUS: Only one guy coulda' done it.

BRUTUS: Yeah? Who?

FLAVIUS: Let's not play games, Brutus—or should I say, Mr. Big.

BRUTUS: What are you gettin' at?

FLAVIUS: If the sandal fits, wear it. You knocked off Big Juli!

BRUTUS: You're out of your head. I hired you to find the killer.

FLAVIUS: Pretty smart, but not smart enough! You gonna talk or do I have to call in a couple of centurions to lean on ya?

BRUTUS: Okay, flatfoot. I did it. I admit it. I knocked off Big Juli—and I'd do it again.

FLAVIUS: That's all I want to know. I'm sending you up the Tiber for a long stretch. Come on, I'll call a chariot, and we'll go downtown.

BRUTUS: Don't move unless you want a dagger in the toga.

FLAVIUS: What?

BRUTUS: I'm gettin' out of here. Don't try to stop me!

FLAVIUS: *(to audience)* He had the drop on me and I couldn't stop him, but I knew where he was heading. For the scene of the crime—the Senate. And 15 minutes later I pulled up in my chariot. Tiberius! Tiberius, hand me the ram's horn.

TIBERIUS: Here you are, Flav.

FLAVIUS: *(cups hands over mouth)* Brutus, this is Flavius Maximus. I know you're in there. Come out with your hands up!

BRUTUS: Hang it on your beak, you dirty rotten flatfoot! Come in and get me!

FLAVIUS: Get smart, Brutus. We can smoke you out. We'll throw incense. We'll throw in an onion on a spear!

BRUTUS: I don't care what you do!

FLAVIUS: You asked for it! Give it to him. Tiberius! *(sound of breaking glass, yelling—then Tiberius emerges from offstage with Brutus)* One false move, Brutus, and I'll fill ya full of bronze!

BRUTUS: You got me, you creep. But I'll be back!

FLAVIUS: Oh no, you won't. This isn't a series.

BRUTUS: Don't worry, I'll be back. Just remember one thing. All roads lead to Rome.

SERGEANT: Come on, you.

FLAVIUS: Hey, wait, wait, wait, wait. Bring him back!

BRUTUS: Huh? What?

FLAVIUS: Wait. Now that one was a dandy!

BRUTUS: What are you talking about?

FLAVIUS: "All roads lead to Rome." That's the best, you know that?

BRUTUS: Do you like it?

FLAVIUS: Yeah, I like it.

BRUTUS: Well, you can't have it.

FLAVIUS: Aw, get out of here!

MAN: Good work, Flavius. All Rome salutes you. Hail, Flavius!

ALL: Hail, Flavius!

FLAVIUS: Thanks, boys. And now if you don't mind, I've got a date with a doll. Okay, baby, I'm ready. Now you're sure your husband doesn't object?

CALPURNIA: Frankly, I don't care. I told him, "Juli, don't go…"

FLAVIUS: Yeah, I know, but maybe we can talk about something else toni—

CALPURNIA: "Juli, don't go," I told him…*(fade out)*

END

SAM SHOVEL, PRIVATE EAR

Here's the first of two announcement skits—skits that make creative lead-ins to an announcement you want to draw particular attention to. Read—or better yet, recite from memory—the monologue on page 44 in your best Clint Eastwood voice. *Steve Smoker*

THE POLITICIAN

Another announcement skit (see "Sam Shovel, Private Ear," page 44). This one begins below. Characters: Emcee, Senator Eustus P. Flatpacker (the one with the announcement), two stagehands, and others (police officers, caterers, etc.—add whatever roles your imagination cooks up, or as many as your stage can hold).

The emcee begins alone onstage with words along these lines:

> Tonight we are pleased to have with us Senator Eustus P. Flatpacker. Mr. Flatpacker is a presidential candidate and is here tonight to present his views on violence in America. Ladies and gentlemen, Senator Eustus P. Flatpacker speaking on violence in America.

Then Flatpacker enters and shakes Emcee's hand. Emcee exits. Flatpacker thanks the audience and begins the event announcement, though with the feel of an election-year speech.

After three or four sentences from the Senator, the stagehands appear in back. Quietly, at first, they argue. A vague argument, such as: "No, I didn't." "Yes, you did." The argument soon heats up. They start shoving each other. One is pushed into the Senator. The Senator continues the announcement as if nothing unusual is happening. All through the skit the Senator is not distracted, continuing as if all was normal.

Dream up really outrageous things for the stagehands to do to the Senator, though it appears that the stagehands are trying to inflict each other with their punishments. Just for starters, stagehand 1 pushes stagehand 2 into the Senator. Stagehand 2 retaliates by pushing the Senator into stagehand 1. If you're outside you can use glasses of water from the podium (or buckets!), whipped cream, etc.

The emcee tries to break it up and is thus brought into the battle. The same happens with a policeman who comes to break it up, with caterers (equipped with pies?), or with a plant from the audience, maybe.

When all the fighting is over, the Senator is still talking. Alone on the stage, his clothes ripped (some ripped off him), sopping wet, covered with whipped cream, he closes his announcement.

The non-announcement variation

What Flatpacker says isn't important—the slapstick action, not an announcement, is what this variation is all about. Flatpacker's speech should be full of pompous language, many-syllable words, and only *start* with a subject relevant to the evening's event—whether graduation, Valentine's Day, or parent night. But gradually the content becomes nonsensical, and all the inflated language gives way to a reading of the Yellow Pages, omelette recipes, *Reader's Digest* excerpts—anything, as long as it's long enough and delivered in a formal, important-sounding style. *John C. Moyer*

SIGHT-GAG SKITS

Here are a half dozen shorties with minimal scripting and maximum opportunities for hamming it up.

• Candy Store

Four kids enter a candy store run by an old man (bent over, shaky voice, beard, and cane) and line up in front of the counter.

First kid asks for a quarter's worth of jelly beans. Old man notices that the jelly beans are on the top shelf and tries to talk her out of it, but the kid insists. So the old man gets a ladder and with much pain climbs to the top, gets the jelly beans, descends the ladder laboriously, exchanges the jelly beans for her quarter, puts the ladder away, then turns to serve the next in line.

The second kid does the same thing—asks for a quarter's worth of jelly beans. Again the old man goes through the same bit, and gets her the jelly beans. He's really slowing down by now.

The third person also asks for a quarter's worth of jelly beans, and the exasperated,

Sam Shovel
PRIVATE EAR

Back in the days of radio there was a famous private eye named Sam Spade. Well, little do you know, but I've been working a second job—and on the streets, they call me Sam Shovel, Private Ear. I'd like to tell you about an average day in the average life of an average private ear. Let's take yesterday, for example.

Yesterday morning I awoke and climbed down off my chandelier—I'm a light sleeper—and headed for my office—my private office. I sat back in my private swivel chair, called for my private secretary, and had her put some of my private Murine in my private eye. Then my eye saw it—a tall, beautiful blonde walked by my office window. She had to be tall—my office is on the third floor.

My phone rang. I picked it up and put the receiver to my private ear. It rang again. Whoops—wrong line. That call was coming in on my private line. I switched lines.

"Hello, Chief...What?...Killer McGurk?...Escaped again?...And you want him back by tonight?...Sounds like a job for Sam Shovel, Private Ear. Chief, I'll get you your man."

I hung up, swiveled my chair around to leave—when suddenly, through the window, I spotted McGurk climbing into a cab across the street. What luck! As I ran out onto the street, I heard the sound of crashing glass behind me. Rats—I'm always forgetting to open that glass door. I hailed a taxi and shouted for him to follow McGurk, but we didn't move. I looked at the cabby—he was shaking all over. It was then I deduced he was a Yellow Cab driver. I leaped into my own car. Ten, 20, 30, 40, 50—60 times I hit the starter. It never did crank. I flagged a Checker cab and lost three games on the roof before we spotted McGurk entering the Grand Hotel. I raced in and questioned the desk clerk.

"Did you see a man come in here with three arms, a pistol in his belt, a knife in his mouth, a sword at his side, a grenade in his hand, one eye in the center of his forehead, and a marble table top strapped to his back?"

"I dunno," the clerk said. "Was there anything unusual about him?"

"Yeah," I replied. "He had a hangnail."

44

"Oh, yeah!" remembered the clerk. "He just went up the stairs."

I took the elevator up to the 50th floor. What a letdown—the building had only 38 stories. After locating the right floor, I proceeded down the hallway. Room 202—empty. Room 204—empty. Room 206—"Sorry, ladies." As I left the ladies room, something grabbed my coattail from behind, pinning me to the wall. I whipped around and delivered a karate chop to the door.

Down the hall I went until I reached room 238. The door swung open—and there stood the most gorgeous three-story blonde I had ever seen. She was the type of woman you could really look up to. She held a machine gun in her hands, clenched a knife between her teeth—but I've seen plenty of James Bond movies and knew exactly what to do. I grabbed old three-story by the arm and laid a kiss right on her lips to cut any quick action she might have planned. But she cut me. The knife, that is. It was still in her mouth.

"I'm looking for McGurk," I growled. "Seen him?"

"Have you checked the clues closet?" she replied smugly.

The clues closet! I should have known! I lunged for the door. She lunged for the door. I lunged. She lunged. We had lunge together that day. Suddenly the door burst open and there stood a man with three arms, a pistol in his belt, a knife in his mouth, a sword at his side, a grenade in his hand, one eye in the center of his forehead, and a marble table top strapped to his back. But I had to make sure. Yup, he had a hangnail, all right.

"Shoot him with your .44!" cried Blondie.

I didn't have a .44, so I shot him twice with my .22—and thus ended the life of Killer McGurk.

I returned to my office to file a report. Suddenly something caught my eye—my private eye. A rock had come flying through my window and hit me in the head. The rock rolled along the floor. I reached for it, but it continued to roll. Hmm—not the first case of rock and roll. Get it—rock 'n' roll? That's a private joke. Anyway, I picked up the rock and noticed a note tied to it. I read the message aloud: **(here read your event announcement)**

END

weary old man climbs up the ladder yet again for the jelly beans. But this time, at the top of the ladder, he asks the last kid, "I guess you want a quarter's worth of jelly beans, too?"

"No," the kid says.

So the old man creaks slowly down (he's wheezing by now) and puts the ladder away yet again.

"Now, what do you want?" he asks.

"I want a dime's worth of jelly beans," the kid says—then runs for his life with the old man in hot pursuit.

• Doctor's Office

An empty waiting room of a doctor's office. A few chairs and magazines. A receptionist seated behind a table.

A man enters and walks to the receptionist. "I'm Mr. Smith," he says. "I have an appointment."

"Fine," he is told. "Please have a seat."

A woman enters, obviously afflicted by a tic—her head snaps violently to the side every three or four seconds. She proceeds to the receptionist, and says, "I'm Ms. Snick. I have an appointment." She is similarly directed to a seat and asked to wait.

After a few moments, Smith's head gives a tic. Then another, and before long Smith is the victim of involuntary neck spasms just like Ms. Snick. Meanwhile, Ms. Snick is getting fewer and fewer tics, until finally she rubs her neck and says with a big smile, "Hey, my problem's gone! Receptionist, cancel my appointment!"

And Smith is twitching like crazy.

And so it goes, each new patient coming in and infecting Smith with yet another—and another, and another—malady, and leaving cured themselves. The maladies can include an arm tic, finger snap, leg kick, etc.

Finally, Smith's head is twitching, his arm is flinging, his leg is kicking, his fingers snapping—and then into the waiting room waddles a very pregnant woman. Smith utters a good old thriller-movie scream and flees the waiting room in horror. *Jim Green*

• Enlarging Machine

Get a large refrigerator box with a hole in it, plus dials, knobs, meters, etc., painted on it like an old-style mainframe computer. Inside the box, concealed from the audience, is your helper—he should be male, the bigger the guy the better.

The creator of the machine, Dr. Cowdungski, demonstrates the machine. He throws a handkerchief into the hole and out comes a sheet...throws in a length of string and out comes a rope...a Ping-Pong ball, and out comes a basketball. Applause follows each demonstration.

Then a female passerby stumbles near the front of the machine, loses her grip on her baby (a doll)—and into the machine it goes.

"Oh, no!" the scientist screams. Then out of the machine bursts the helper—in diapers with a bottle, shouting, "Mommy!" *Lawrence Fitzpatrick*

• Hey, Dumbrowski!

It's wartime, and a firefight is under way. Behind each of two facing barricades a few feet apart, four soldiers are shooting away at their enemy. For the sake of explaining this skit, call them the red and blue armies.

A blue soldier yells over the barricade to the red army, "Hey, Finkbeiner!"

Finkbeiner stands up, unprotected, and says, "Yeah, what do you want?" The blue army then shoots Finkbeiner and he falls.

Another blue soldier calls over, "Hey, Klutzenberg!" Klutzenberg on the red side stands up and says, "Yes, did you call me?" He gets shot.

Again, a blue soldier calls out: "Hey, Farnsworthy!" Farnsworthy stands up, answers, and gets shot like the others.

Now, the only red soldier left is Dumbrowski, who scratches his head and says, "Ha, I get it! They call out our names, we stand up, and then they shoot us. Well, we can play that little game, too!"

So Dumbrowski yells out to the blue side, "Hey, Smith!" to which a blue soldier does not stand, but yells back, "Hey, is that you Dumbrowski?" Dumbrowski then stands up and says, "Yeah, it's me!"—and gets shot.

• Future Banana

This short skit is perfect for those in-between moments—between acts in a talent show, between main segments of an event, etc. An actor simply walks out on stage, sits on a chair in the middle of the stage, and takes out a banana. Meanwhile, in the background plays the opening movement from "Thus Spake Zerathustra"—the musical theme from the movie *2001: A Space Odyssey*. The actor then eats the banana, doing her best to synchronize the peeling and eating of it to the music. If done properly, with slo-mo, exaggerated expressions, the results are hilarious. *Steve Siverns and Tim Criuckshanks*

• Great Piano Recital

For this musical skit you need an upright piano, a spinet piano (an upright is taller than a spinet), a good pianist, and a good actor. Put the upright piano on stage, keyboard side squarely facing the audience. Then hide the shorter spinet piano behind it so that the audience can't see it. Have the real pianist out of everyone's sight at the spinet piano and the actor at the upright piano. The actor should be a person known for his musical inability.

Announce to the audience that a guest pianist is going to entertain everyone. Then have the audience write song requests on slips of paper which are collected. The guest pianist—that is, the unmusical actor—should read the name of the request and then ham it

up as if he was really playing it, while a real pianist on the spinet is actually playing. It gets really funny when the visible pianist guesses where the next notes will be on the piano keyboard. *Dallas Elder*

SPONTANEOUS MELODRAMAS

Dated? Absolutely. Corny? You bet. But these no-rehearsal, no-prep melodramatic spoofs can bring down the house. If your actors are willing to overact to the max—fueled by groans, catcalls, cheers, and boos from the audience—then they'll finish to thunderous applause. Beginning this collection of spontaneous melodramas is a helpful explanation of just what they are and how to perform them for the most effect.

What are spontaneous melodramas, anyway?

They are exciting and creative ways to get students moving around, learning, and laughing—especially if the spontaneous melodrama is a Bible story. We've just never heard kids complain (*"That's so boring"*) after doing melodramas like these with them.

Simply put, a spontaneous melodrama is a humorous narrative reading, during which actors dramatize the narrative's action—with melodramatic exaggeration, and on the spot, with no rehearsals.

It looks like this: you call the requisite number of teenagers up front, assign them their roles—animate or inanimate—and instruct them to do whatever you read. If you read that the trees wave furiously in gale-force winds, then the student trees do their best to wave furiously. If the protagonist is said to weep buckets, the student actor wails loudly—and the more melodramatic, the better.

Such overacting won't score with their high school drama instructor, but it's hilarious in a slapstick sort of way. Plus it makes the event, the evening, the meeting—or the Bible lesson—memorable.

Take these spontaneous melodramas with you on a retreat. Use them on Saturday night. Use them on Sunday morning. Let them introduce an announcement, a party, or a Bible lesson.

So here are a few things to remember when doing spontaneous melodramas with youth groups:
- **Add some planning to the spontaneity.** "Planned spontaneity"? Well, yes, kind of. A little preparation is quality control for your otherwise spontaneous production. In fact, at the beginning of each script are leader hints, which are suggestions we've found useful for performing that melodrama.

The *timing* of your reading and *casting* are everything. About timing: the humor can take a completely different turn (or drop out altogether) with different timing and delivery of a line. So be sure to read the melodrama through at least once, looking for places in the script which need your particular attention—where you can make or break the line.

As far as casting goes, select kids with personalities that will enhance the role. Some very general suggestions are implicit in the cast lists at the beginning of each script. Just be careful and use your discernment: you don't want a student with a weight problem playing the part of a whale. Enough said.
- **Mind your pauses and cues.** When a line you read calls for action, pause long enough for the actors to act. No need to race through the scripts. Take your time!

• **Tweak the scripts.** If the script calls for ten people and you have only five, rewrite it. Have students play more than one role. Not enough males in your group for a melodrama? Go ahead and use females. Alter the scripts however it best suits your group. Take all the poetic license you want in the narration, for a spontaneous melodrama's narration is as crucial as its acting.

Season your reading with impromptu comments and fillers. For example, if your actor doesn't deliver a line with sufficient enthusiasm, say something like "...and because Trueheart said his words so apathetically, the audience booed him until he spoke with conviction and enthusiasm." Is his delivery *still* lackluster? "...Finally, with the audience silent as snow, Trueheart screamed the words as if all the world could hear them..."

Or if this or that action or gesture is a big hit, capitalize on it by adding impromptu: "She kept dancing in circles until the audience counted to five."

Or if your bench or boat or boulder gets the giggles: "And the tree jumped from behind the bush and covered Jeanette's mouth so the audience could hear the rest of this melodrama." You get the idea.

• **Make it big.** The bigger, the broader, the more hyperbolic the action, the better. Get your kids thinking big falls, rubber faces, oversized movements and loud-loud-loud exclamations. Encourage your students to go all-out! They'll have more fun doing it—and everyone will have more fun watching it.

• **Beware: Some of these melodramas ain't mellow.** We admit it: now and then in these scripts you'll find isolated, infrequent instances of gratuitous nose-pickings, hand-in-armpit noises, and—shall we say—creative liberty with Bible stories. On the other hand, it doesn't take an M.Div. to conclude that such unmellow spontaneous melodramas probably aren't appropriate for Sunday morning worship services. So change what you must to suit your group; you know the written and unwritten guidelines of taste in your church or youth group.

Furthermore, these are action scripts. Not much subtlety here. So you may want to rearrange your room some to allow for the action—especially since even the audience plays an active role in many of the scripts. After all, your goal is to get as many people as possible involved. And when you do a spontaneous melodrama, you may want to warn the Twilighters, the toddlers, or whatever Sunday school class is next door to the youth room: it may get a little, ah, boisterous.

Then again, they're probably used to it by now.

Adapted from Spontaneous Melodramas: 24 Impromptu Skits That Bring Bible Stories to Life by Doug Fields, Laurie Polich, and Duffy Robbins. Copyright 1996 by Youth Specialties.

✦　✦　✦

PARABLE OF THE GOOD SAMARITAN

This spontaneous melodrama, based on Luke 10:30-36, is on page 53. Take your cues from this for rewriting just about any Bible story into a spontaneous melodrama like this one. *Barry Kolanowski*

AS THE STOMACH ACID BURNS

Use this four-act melodrama (that begins on page 54) for a weekend retreat or to kick off each of four consecutive youth meetings. You can use the same group of actors for all four acts, or four different sets of actors. *Carlton S. Deal*

THE RICH FOOL

Based on the parable in Luke 12:16-21, this spontaneous melodrama is not only humorous to watch, but it can be a discussion starter about materialism, consumerism, possessions, etc. Explore the subject with your students with questions like these:
• How important is it to you and your school friends to have the "right" things or possessions?
• Why do you think our society is so stuck on things?
• What priority have you lately given to seeking first God's kingdom?
• Describe some of the difficulties you face in storing up treasure in heaven versus storing up treasure on earth.
• Brainstorm realistic ideas that could help you to become rich toward God. List these ideas.
• Choose one idea from the list that you will try this week in order to escape the trap of materialism.

The script begins on page 58. *Jim Liebelt*

Good Samaritan

CHARACTERS
•Narrator •Traveler •3 Gangsters
•Priest •Levite •Samaritan

NARRATOR: One day a goodly traveler was strolling along humming to himself, thinking everything was fine. When all of a sudden out of the rocks jumped three of the meanest gangsters you've ever seen. They had beady eyes and they would grind their teeth together. They started to beat on the traveler, then all at once two of them grabbed his arms while the other started to punch him. When the action seemed to freeze, the traveler remembered and said to himself, "I know Kung Fu!" And he broke free and started to fight back. But the gangsters knocked him down to the ground. But on the way down to the ground *(chances are, he's already on the ground—but repeat the words "But on the way down" until he gets up)*, he let out a loud and terrible shout, followed by a deep grunt. The thieves grabbed his money and split, yelling and leaping for joy.

As he lay there a'groanin' and moanin', along came a priest who, when seeing the man, was shocked, and walked around him saying, "I am shocked but it serveth him righteth, for traveling aloneth."

Then came a Levite, and the man is still groaning. When the Levite saw and heard him, he ran to the side of the man and said, "Oh my, oh my, what a pity!" And he started to help the man up, but then noticed what time it was and dropped the man. The man lets out a scream. The Levite said, "I am lateth for worship at the synagogueth—must not let man come beforeth God." And he walks away.

And finally comes along a Samaritan who when seeing the man is moved with compassion, and comes over to bandage the man, then helps him up, but slips on a wet stone and drops him. After a lot of strain, he picks the man up and carries him to town.

END

AS THE
Stomach Acid Burns

CHARACTERS
•Narrator •Polly Pureheart •Granny Griselda •Byron the Biceps •Tyrone the Triceps
•Fred the Fat •Pup the Dog •Table (2 actors) •Chair (actor)

PROPS
•Cutesy dress for Polly •Shawl • Wig •Toy machine-gun •Bandolier of machine-gun ammunition •Long rope
•Muscle shirts for Byron and Tyrone •Cushion of fake stomach for Fred •Box of chocolates •Dog ears and nose

ACT 1

NARRATOR: It is with great pride that I introduce <u>As the Stomach Acid Burns</u>, performed by the First Church Players. First, the characters:

Polly Pureheart, still saddened by the mysterious disappearance of her husband, Paul Pureheart, is contemplating marriage once again. She lives with her not-so-sweet and not-so-lovely grandmother.

Granny Griselda has not been mellowed by time. She has wrinkles on her wrinkles, especially on her hog-slopping muscles, which is why she needs Polly, who is the best hog-slopper in the whole U.S. of A.

Polly is being courted by three handsome, bungling idiots—Byron the Biceps, Tyrone the Triceps, and Fred the Fat—who, unfortunately, has Dunlop's disease: his belly has done lopped over his belt.

Polly is often comforted by her faithful dog, Pup, whose name spelled backward is, significantly, Pup.

Oh, yes—and our table and chair. They have important supporting roles.

Now, on with the first of four acts.

As our story opens, we find lovely Polly Pureheart in her Grandma's house, where she's lived since her husband, Paul

Pureheart, mysteriously disappeared. Polly is sitting comfortably on the chair with her legs propped up on the table. With one hand she is scratching Pup's head, for which Pup energetically wags his tail. With her other hand, she's plucking her one eyebrow. She used to have two, but a shaving accident cost her the other one.

Granny Griselda jumps into the room, accidentally landing on Pup's tail. Pup yelps and hides under the table. "I told you to slop them hogs!" says Granny in her shrill, scratchy voice. She turns and stomps out of the room.

Suddenly there's a knock at the door. Pup barks, drooling all over himself with excitement. "Come in," answers Polly in her husky voice. In bounds Byron the Biceps, flexing his, and Tyrone the Triceps, touching his toes—and Fred the Fat, eating chocolate.

Byron says, "Polly, I will climb the highest mountain for your hand in marriage."

Tyrone says, "Polly, I will swim the deepest ocean for your hand in marriage."

Fred says, "Wanna piece of chocolate?"

To prove their strength, Byron and Tyrone decide to have an arm wrestling match on the table, while Fred excitedly eats chocolate. After a short but intense struggle, which attracts Granny's attention, Byron wins the match. Fred releases a congratulatory belch, which reminds Granny of the unslopped hogs. She stomps in and threatens, "Polly, if you don't slop them hogs, I'll cut you up and feed you to them for dinner!"

Polly's mouth drops open with horror—and stays that way for the remainder of the act. Byron, Tyrone, and Fred begin to laugh—until Granny pulls out her automatic and throws off her shawl to reveal a bandolier of machine-gun ammo. "Call me Grambo," she shrieks in her shrill, scratchy voice. At this Byron, Tyrone, and Fred scream and frantically head for the door, each of them tripping over the table and then the dog on their way out. Granny smiles an evil smile, knowing that she has a hog-slopper for life, unless...

Come back tomorrow, when you'll hear Granny say: "Go ahead—make my day."

ACT 2

NARRATOR: Good evening, ladies and gents. We proudly present Act 2 of <u>As the Stomach Acid Burns</u>, performed by the First Church Players.

When we last saw poor Polly Pureheart, she had been ruthlessly threatened and now held captive by her evil Granny Griselda for her refusal to slop the hogs. As we resume our story, we find that poor Polly's mouth is still open with horror at her fate—and remains open for the duration of the act. Granny is still smiling her evil smile.

Granny laughs a shrill, sinister laugh, then begins tying Polly to the chair and her legs to the top of the table. At this Polly begins wailing loudly (and continues until told to stop). Then she starts a kicking fit right on top of the table. The table withstands much of the kicking, but finally collapses. Granny finishes tying Polly up, then stomps out—leaving in the room only Polly tied up and wailing, a collapsed table, and

Polly's faithful dog Pup—which, significantly, spells Pup backward.

This same Pup, intuitively sensing Polly's frustration, disappointment, confusion, anxiety, sadness, pain, and general discomfort, barks a few reassuring barks to the tune of "Jingle Bells." Polly stops her wailing, but—still melancholy about her life sentence of pig-slopping—says, "Hmpf." Pup wags his tail and ponders other ways of cheering her. First he crawls over the wreckage of the table and licks her feet. No luck—Polly is still overwhelmed with frustration, disappointment, confusion, anxiety, sadness, pain, and general discomfort. He then licks her arm, from her hand to her shoulder. Finally, convinced that a wet nose is a happy nose, Pup presses his cold, wet nose against Polly's warm, dry nose. Polly, unimpressed, pushes Pup—whose name spelled backward is, significantly, Pup—onto the ruins of the table.

Just then comes a knock at the door. In bounds Byron the Biceps, Tyrone the Triceps, and Fred the Fat. They all say in unison, and with great feeling, "We have come to rescue you, dear Polly." Byron the Biceps says, "I will climb the highest mountain for your hand in marriage." Tyrone the Triceps says, "I will swim the deepest ocean for your hand in marriage." Fred the Fat says, "Wanna piece of chocolate?"

Polly squeals in delight. "Oh, my big strong men—and Fred!" she exclaims. And finally forsaking her mysteriously disappeared husband, Polly says, in her husky voice, "I will marry the man who rescues me from my grandmother." Immediately they all three jump on the broken table and try to untie her legs—which, of course, tickles the table and causes it to laugh.

But right then Granny Griselda stomps back into the room. The men and Fred freeze in their rescue attempt. Granny lowers her automatic at them, then again reveals her ammo belts. "Now I'm gonna have to feed you to the hogs, too," she says in her shrill, scratchy voice. The men and Fred begin to wail uncontrollably, begging for mercy on their knees and kissing all 10 of Granny's toes one by one.

But Granny simply smiles her wicked smile. Grambo has captured them all. How will they be saved from the flesh-eating hogs? Come back tomorrow, when you'll hear Granny say: "Them hogs sure are hungry."

ACT 3

NARRATOR: Howdy, again. Here we are with Act 3 of As the Stomach Acid Burns, performed by the First Church Players.

When we last saw poor Polly Pureheart, the men, and Fred, they were all ensnared by the evil Granny Griselda. One can't help but wonder how they will be saved from the man-eating hogs. Still smiling her evil smile, Granny reminds us, "Them hogs sure are hungry."

As our story resumes, we find Polly wailing uncontrollably and beating on the chair, Byron wailing uncontrollably and beating on Tyrone, and Tyrone wailing uncontrollably and beating on Byron—and Fred eating chocolate. Pup—which, significantly, spells Pup backward—scampers under the table—which, amazingly, has been reassembled—for shelter from all the wailing, which continues in unison.

Granny laughs her infamous, sinister laugh, which quiets everyone. She begins to tie Polly, the men, and Fred together. Polly does not put up a fight and is tied up easily. She returns to plucking her one eyebrow and eating the hairs.

Byron the Biceps, however, refuses to be tied up. Shaking his head vigorously, he stands up and announces, "I will climb the highest mountain for Polly's hand." He begins flexing his muscles and doing Arnold Schwarzenegger poses. He runs in place for 10 seconds, does 12 jumping jacks, drops to the floor for 10 push-ups, then jumps to his

feet, flexes once more—then falls over, exhausted. Granny ties him up.

Tyrone the Triceps is also struggling against being tied up. He lets out a war whoop, bounds to this feet, and starts a series of energetic toe-touches. As he bends over for his ninth toe-touch, Granny kicks him in his derriere and he falls over onto the table, which again collapses, this time on Pup—which, interestingly enough, spells Pup backward. Pup yelps loudly. Granny ties Tyrone up.

Fred, meanwhile, doesn't mind at all being tied up. He just wants to eat his chocolate. Granny ties him up, laughs her sinister laugh, then stomps out of the room—leaving her captives all wailing uncontrollably.

Without warning, however, Granny stomps back into the room, snatches Fred's box of chocolates, and turns to stomp out again.

But not before Fred the Fat comes to life with a vengeance. With one swift motion, he unties himself. He jumps up and down like a wild man, throws off the burden of his extra weight, beats his chest, and bellows like Tarzan. The mouths of Granny, Polly, Byron, Tyrone, and Pup drop open in amazement—and stay that way for the remainder of the act. Fred roars, "I WANT MY CANDY!" then races for Granny and grabs her by the throat.

Will Fred save the day? Will the hogs stay hungry after all? Return tomorrow when the mouths of Granny, Polly, Byron, Tyrone, and Pup will still be hanging open.

ACT 4

NARRATOR: For the last time, ladies and gents, good evening. We welcome you to the exciting conclusion of As the Stomach Acid Burns, performed by our own First Church Players.

When we left the home of the wicked Granny Griselda, Granny had made the fatal mistake of stealing Fred's box of chocolates. Before our very eyes, Fred the Fat threw off his excess weight and became a virtual wild man. All hope is not yet lost.

As the curtain rises on our concluding act, the table is still broken. The chair, however, is smiling—for he knows the story is almost over. Fred is breathing deeply, heavily, and loudly. The mouths of Granny, Polly, Byron, and Tyrone are still hanging open in amazement at Fred's ferocious feats. (Pup—which, interestingly enough, spells Pup backward—has closed his mouth because Polly told him backstage that he had bad breath.)

Like an uncontrollable beast Fred springs toward Granny, runs around her three times, bellows an ear-splitting Tarzan yell, then bites Granny's nose. Polly, Tyrone, Byron, Pup—which, when spelled upside down, interestingly enough, is dnd—and the entire audience chant, "Go, Fred! Go, Fred!" Fred tears off Granny's wig, and the audience responds with a cheer. When Fred laughs Granny's wicked laugh, grabs a piece of the collapsed table, swings it over his shoulder, and slowly stalks toward Granny, the audience goes crazy. Granny, sore-nosed and wigless, her whole body shaking with fear, drops onto her knees and begs for mercy. But nothing arrests Fred's inexorable pursuit of that evil woman. As her last hope she grabs the box of chocolates and offers it to Fred. At the sight of his precious chocolates, Fred drops the table piece, grabs the chocolates, smiles his fat, hungry-for-chocolate smile, ties himself up, and begins to munch his chocolates contentedly.

Their hopes crushed, Polly, Byron, Tyrone, Pup—which, significantly, is spelled dnd upside down—and the entire audience wail uncontrollably. Fred continues eating chocolate. Granny gets up, puts her wig back in place, powders her nose, then laughs her sinister laugh. In her shrill, scratchy voice she says, "Now, to slop them hogs!" All wail even louder, their bodies shaking with fear.

Then Pup comes to life. He switches his tail ominously and growls a throaty, menacing growl. Granny levels her automatic at him, but Pup grabs it between his teeth, tussles the gun out of her hands, and tosses it into the audience. With a gleam in his eye, Pup rises on his hind legs, and with his broad, red, slobbery tongue, licks all over Granny's face—first her chin, then both cheeks, then bites her nose. To everyone's amazement Granny starts screaming and shriveling up like a salted slug. The mouths of the audience drop open in horror and remain that way for the remainder of the act. In her shrill, sinister voice, Granny shrieks, "I'm melting! I'm melting! I'm...dead..."

Pup has saved the day. Everyone cheers (with their mouths still hanging open). Pup unties Polly, Byron, Tyrone, and Fred. Polly picks up Pup and says, "Oh, Pup—which significantly, spells Pup backward—you're my hero!" and kisses Pup on the nose.

Suddenly Pup stands up on two legs and takes off his ears, then his nose. Polly finds herself looking into a pair of familiar brown eyes, and exclaims in her husky voice, "Paul Pureheart!"

You see, the wicked Granny Griselda had turned Polly's husband Paul into a dog so she could keep Polly forever. "Paul," said Polly. "Polly," said Paul. "Paul, Paul" said Polly. "Polly, Polly," said Paul. "Paul, Paul, Paul," said Polly. "Polly, Polly, Polly," said Paul. They continue this as they walk out, staring into each other's eyes.

Which leaves Byron the Biceps, Tyrone the Triceps, and Fred the Fat. Byron says, "But I would have climbed the highest mountain for Polly's hand." Tyrone says, "And I would have swum the deepest ocean for Polly's hand."

Fred says, "I sure have eaten a lot of chocolate—and my stomach acid burns."

END

The Rich Fool

CHARACTERS
•Narrator •Rich man •Barn (2 people) •New wood for the barn (2 more people)
•Crop (2 people) •Easy chair (1 person) •Workers (2 big, strong guys) •God

NARRATOR: Jesus told this parable (well, his parable was sort of like this):

Once there was a rich man who went out into his field one day to look at this crop. He was very fond of his crop. You could tell he was fond of his crop because he would look over his crop lovingly. He would touch his crop. He would smell his crop—even though he was allergic to his crop. So whenever he smelled his crop, he sneezed on it. This made the crop sway back and forth. As he looked over his swaying crop, he would sneeze and say, "What a great crop!"

Then he said, "But what shall I do? My barn is too small for my crop!" Disappointed, he walked over and kicked the barn—which only injured his foot. He hopped around in pain, his face contorted by the anguish. Then he said, "I know...I'll hire workers to tear down this old barn and build me a bigger barn."

So that's what he did. The workers came out and tried tearing down the old barn. But the barn was strong and resisted. No matter how hard the workers tried to demolish the barn, it just kept on standing there. Yet the workers finally prevailed; the barn reluctantly yielded to the efforts of the workers. The old building crumbled—right on top of the workers. After a long struggle, however, the workers were able to squeeze out from underneath the ruins of the old barn.

Next, the workers carried in new wood to make a bigger barn. But they ran out of new wood—so they used the wood of the old barn to finish the new, bigger barn. The only problem was that the wood from the old barn was very heavy and was difficult to put into place.

Once the new barn was in place, the rich man said to his workers, "Hey, guys—nice barn." Then he said, "Why don't you come out and help me bring in my crop?"

"We'll do it!" said the workers.

"Great!" said the rich man. "This way, guys." The rich man turned and hopped off toward the field. The workers followed the rich man, also hopping as they went. When they were in the field, the rich man showed them his beautiful crop. He told them to touch the crop. He told them to smell the crop. The workers, also allergic to the crop, also sneezed on it. The crop swayed in the wind.

"Well, boys," said the rich man. "Take my crop into the barn." So the workers picked up the crop and carried it into the barn, sneezing all the way along and causing the crop to sway back and forth—which made it difficult to carry.

Once the crop was safely in the barn and the workers had gone home for the night (sneezing all the way home), the rich man said to himself, "Now I have plenty of good things. This stuff will last me for many years. I can take life easy. I'll eat, drink, and be merry."

With that, he reclined in his easy chair. But for some reason the easy chair was wobbly. The rich man tried to get comfortable, but he couldn't. Suddenly the chair collapsed under the weight of the rich man.

He hit his head on the floor and passed out.

In a dream he saw God stand above him and say, "Yo, rich dude. You be a fool. This night you gonna die. Then who's gonna own all that stash of yours?"

The next morning the workers sneezed their way to work—and found the dead man. They gasped. They sneezed. They carried him to the barn and threw him in among the swaying crop.

The moral of the story? It's in Luke 12:21: "This is how it will be with anyone who stores up things for himself but is not rich toward God."

END

Greek Tragedy in Nine Acts

In this spontaneous melodrama, you (or the narrator) is just about the only one with any lines (the Page has four words). The fun, though, is in the goofy, overacted death scenes hammed up by eight people. Make the costumes as ridiculous as possible. A final comic touch: reverse the genders for some of the roles. For instance, cast a boy in the role of Little Nell, a girl in the role of Colonel, etc. The script is on page 61.

The Seagull and the Surfer

Remember, in a spontaneous melodrama even actors playing inanimate objects—like ocean waves—get in on the hammy action ("The waves rise in great swells."). "The Seagull and the Surfer" begins on page 62. *Cathy Crone*

A Lake Excursion

No rehearsals are necessary for this audience-participation skit. The narrator's part begins on page 63. It's based on Mark 4:35-41, which describes the Galilee sailing jaunt during which Jesus slept through a storm. This skit makes an effective springboard for a study of the Mark passage or for topical discussions about adolescent pressures and stress. *Molly Halter*

Parable of the Great Banquet

This spontaneous melodrama is a fun retelling of Christ's parable in Luke 14:16-24. Choose the hams in your group to play these characters extravagantly—especially the Great Man. If possible, give the script (which begins on page 65) to the narrator prior to the performance so she can read it through a couple times so that she gets the proper timing. *Kathryn L. Zucker*

Penelope's Predicament

Warm up your audience with some melodramatic practice: have them clap and cheer wildly every time they hear Studley Storm's name or every time he comes on stage. When Snidely Whiplash appears or is mentioned, they should boo and hiss. Penelope Pureheart receives fond, feminine oohs and aahs. The script begins on page 67. *Mark Henjum*

Perils of the Prodigal

This spontaneous melodrama is actually the parable of the Prodigal Son. Remember—the more exaggerated the acting, the more effective the skit! The script is on page 69. *Mark Frost*

Two Blind Men

Here's a humorous retelling of Matthew 20:29-34. Make sure your audience interacts with your on-the-spot actors with cheers, hisses, and boos. The script is on page 72. *Bill Splawn*

GREEK TRAGEDY
in Nine Acts

CHARACTERS

- MacBeth (prince with cape, hat, etc.)

- Lady MacBeth (in old woman's clothing, including a stole and hat)

- Juliet (perhaps carrying flowers)

- Marie Antoinette (rig it to make her look headless)

- Little Nell (a little girl)

- Page (boy or girl)

- Colonel (equipped with hat, boots, sword, etc.)

- Gunga Din (boy, shirtless and shoeless, in jeans, scarf on head)

- Narrator

PROPS

•Cap gun (for narrator) •Simulated head on a platter—a mask on a cantaloupe works just fine (for Page)

NARRATOR: A greek tragedy in nine acts. Nine acts because everybody has to get into the act. Greek because your guess is as good as ours. Tragedy because we're all just dying to do it. I will introduce the cast of characters in order of their appearance.

(read in a poetic style)

MacBeth made a desperate stand for his life,
But was finally murdered by a plot of his wife.

(enter MacBeth who drops dead)

Lady MacBeth soon went to pot.
She lost her head over that "damned spot."

(enter Lady MacBeth who drops dead as if gone mad)

The train ran over little Nell.
It blew its whistle and rang its bell.
It mashed her up, so they tell,
And that's the last of little Nell.

(she enters and drops dead)

Juliet...she and her lover were torn apart,
And so she died of a broken heart.

(she enters and dies)

Marie Antoinette, the Queen of France,
Had diamonds, pearls, and a jewelled clock.
But she lost her head on a chopping block.

(she enters headless, falls over dead)

Many heads rolled but few in the clatter
Have ever been seen on a silver platter.

(Page enters and stands still, holding the head)

A trace of lavender and a dab of lace
The Colonel stubbed his toe and fell on his face.

(he charges in, stubs toe, and falls down dead)

Water, water, cried Gunga Din.
He was gallant and brave, but just couldn't win.

(he enters gasping for water, dies)

Now we are ready to begin our play, but we regret that due to circumstances beyond our control, the cast being dead, we'll be unable to perform tonight.

PAGE BOY: Hey, what about me?

NARRATOR: Drop dead.

(pulls out the cap gun and shoots him)

END

The Seagull and the Surfer

A Spontaneous Melodrama

CHARACTERS

•Narrator •Sun •Seagulls (any number) •Waves (any number) •Surfer •Shore (any number)

NARRATOR: It is a bright and beautiful morning at the beach. The sun is slowly rising, and the seagulls are waking up after a long night's rest; the waves are calm and serene and the shore is smooth and damp.

The ocean world now seems to come alive as the seagulls chatter to each other and fly off on their morning search for food. As the gulls are flying over the shore and waves, they begin to get playful. They soar higher and higher, then drop suddenly skimming the waves with their outstretched wings. They fly up, then up, then up and down again, in circles, in zigzags, backward, then forward. The gulls are chattering noisily, screaming as loud as they can. Suddenly, the playfulness ends and the gulls return slowly to their nests to rest.

The waves are beginning to rise in great swells. They rise higher and higher reaching farther and farther until at the last second they come crashing down on each other and roll on to the shore.

A surfer arrives at the beach, stepping on the shore. Excited at the prospect of the big waves that are continuing to break on the shore, the surfer begins to jump up and down. He sits on the shore and gazes at the breaking waves.

The surfer now decides to take his board out into the water. He paddles out, making fast, long strokes. He paddles faster and faster with longer and harder strokes until he reaches the point where he is past the waves. He uses his skill to dodge in and out of the waves with precision timing. He is full of poise and grace as he "hangs ten" on his surfboard. Then suddenly a wave grabs him and sends him crashing into the shore.

The surfer, now tired and beaten, gathers up his surfboard and slowly stumbles away from the shore and heads for home.

The day is coming to an end as the sun slowly sets. The birds make their last flight for the day flying over the shore and waves and once again return to their nests for a cozy night's sleep, tucking their wings under their bodies and lowering their heads.

As we take one last look at the beautiful ocean scene before the sun sets, we can see the restful seagulls, and the waves beating on the shore.

END

A Lake Excursion

A SPONTANEOUS MELODRAMA

CHARACTERS

•Narrator •Disciples (12 people) •Jesus •Boat (8-12 people) •Sail •Cushion •Wind (4-5 people) •Waves (4-5 people)

NARRATOR: Jesus and his disciples had spent a long day of teaching and preaching by the lake and evening had come. Jesus said to the disciples, "Let's go over to the other side of the lake and find a McDonald's." With great enthusiasm, everyone said, "Yeah!" and rapidly nodded their heads up and down. They were all so dog-tired they were hanging onto each other in order to stand up. They all climbed into the boat.

Jesus was tired too, of course. He climbed in the boat, walked directly to the back, lay his head down on the cushion, and immediately began snoring.

The tiny fishing boat set out from shore, rocking gently in the quiet waters of Lake Galilee. While Jesus snored the disciples leaned against the sides of the boat, laughing and talking. The wind swayed softly over the lake, and the boat's sail gently followed the direction of the little breezes. The waves sweetly lapped the sides of the boat.

And everyone was thinking of a Big Mac, fries, and a chocolate shake, to go.

But out of nowhere came a furious squall. *(At this point the narrator asks the audience to stomp their feet and clap their hands to provide sound effects for the storm)* The waves broke over the sides of the boat. The sail swung around and around on the mast, bonking the disciples on their heads. The wind and the waves rocked the boat madly—its occupants were pitched first to one side of the boat, and then to the other. And still the sail swung around, bonking more disciples. The boat continued heaving—and soon the disciples were, too, leaning over the sides of the boat. It got gross.

Finally in desperation, one of the disciples recovered enough to grab the sail and hang on to it, to keep it from swinging around and bonking more people on the head. Though he was still seasick, he hung onto that sail. The poor sail was a mess.

But in the back of the boat, the pitching only put Jesus into a deeper sleep—and produced louder snores. The cushion rocked, too, of course, but it didn't snore.

The disciples wildly scrambled around and over each another in desperation. Some began bailing. Others shouted to each other questions like "Where's Jesus?" "Can't he help us?" "What's he doing?"

So on their hands and knees, they all crawled to the back of the boat and surrounded Jesus, who was still sleeping peacefully, snoring, rocking gently, his head on the cushion.

Together the disciples shouted to Jesus, "Teacher! Don't you care if we drown?" They shouted it again, in unison this time, because they didn't do it too well the first time.

Finally, Jesus rolled over, sat up on top of the cushion, yawned, and rubbed his eyes. "Hey, what's up?" he asked sleepily.

It only took him a moment to grasp the desperate situation, so he got up and walked to the middle of the boat. Here he could view everything—the stressed-out disciples, the rocking boat, the sail still thrashing about, the crashing waves, the violent wind. He stretched out his arms and cried out in a loud voice, "Waves! Be still!"

Immediately, the waves fell flat on their faces outside the boat and lay still, as good waves should do. Then Jesus cried out again, "Wind! Die down!"

Immediately the wind died down all over on top of the waves and lay still on top of the waves like good wind should do.

The boat stopped rocking, the sail stopped spinning about, and everything was calm, quiet, and just plain cool. Jesus looked over everything, looked at the wind, the waves, the boat, the sail, the cushion—even the disciples. He looked at the disciples a long time. He looked first at one, than at another—at all of them, one at a time.

Finally he said softly, "Why are you so afraid? Do you still have no faith?"

The disciples, still terrified and huddled together, said to each other, "Who is this man? Even the wind and waves obey him!"

But then the disciples all breathed a huge, loud sigh of relief. A very huge, loud sigh. Then they jumped up and hugged Jesus and thanked him. All at once. Big group hug. And the little fishing boat sailed calmly to the other side of the lake, sail flapping happily in the wind.

When they landed, the disciples climbed out of the boat, safe and sound, and decided to go, not to McDonald's after all, but to Subway instead.

END

PARABLE OF

The Great Banquet

CHARACTERS
•Narrator •Great Man •Trusty Dog •First servant •Second servant
•Third servant •Farmer Fiona •Joe, the used ox salesman •Groom

NARRATOR: This is the story of Great Man. He walked around proudly with his chest out, frequently thumping it with great delight. Following close behind him was Trusty Dog. Great Man accidently stepped on Trusty Dog. Great Man was very bored and was wandering around his great house trying to decide what to do. He stroked his beard, tapped his forehead, and once again stepped on the dog.

"I've got it!" he exclaimed, jumping in the air. "I will prepare a great feast and invite many guests. Yes!" Great Man exclaimed as he pumped his fist in the air, petted Trusty Dog on his head, and accidently stepped on him. Trusty Dog bit Great Man.

"I must find my servants!" Great Man yelled. Immediately three servants ran into his presence and they each stepped on Trusty Dog. Trusty Dog growled, snarled, and once again decided to bite Great Man on the leg...but he didn't.

"You bellowed, sir?" the three servants asked.

"I did," Great Man replied. "I have prepared a great banquet. You must tell those I invited that everything is now ready."

"As you wish," replied the first servant.

"As you wish," replied the second servant.

"Yeah, whatever," the third servant replied.

Off they went, skipping through the kingdom, looking for guests of Great Man. They were happily skipping along, humming a tune, when the first servant ran into Farmer Fiona.

(In his best drawl) "Howdy Farmer Fiona!" said the first servant. "It's time to come to the Great Feast."

"I'm sorry," sighed Farmer Fiona, "but I just bought a field, and I must go and see it. See ya!" Farmer Fiona left singing "When the Saints Go Marchin' In" as loudly as she could.

Once again the three servants skipped around town looking for the guests of Great Man. All of a sudden the second servant tripped on something in the road. They looked down, and who could it be but Joe, the used ox salesman. Joe, the used ox salesman, got up, brushed himself off, and pushed the second servant. The second servant was going to push Joe, the used ox salesman back—but at the last second, he didn't.

"Joe, the used ox salesman," the second servant said. "It's time to go to the Great Feast."

"Ahh," sighed Joe, the used ox salesman. "I can't. I'm taking oxen on a test run today." Stomping his feet and dancing a little jig, Joe, the used ox salesman, left.

The three servants continued skipping along when the third servant, who is very sensitive, started crying. "There must be a wedding around somewhere," blubbered the third servant. "I can't seem to stop crying."

Just then the groom, tall and handsome, walked up to the third servant, and in his most proper British accent, asked, "What are you doing blubbering at my wedding?"

"I'm here to tell you the Great Feast is ready," said the third servant as he blew his nose on the groom's jacket. The groom pushed the third servant away." I can't attend the Great Feast. I just got married." The groom stalked off with his nose high in the air.

The three servants were very sad. Their feet dragged all the way back to Great Man. As they entered the great hall, the third servant accidently kicked Trusty Dog, who growled and bit Great Man, who hit Trusty Dog, who licked the first servant's hand.

Great Man was very angry when he heard that no one was able to attend the Great Feast. He sent the three servants out all over the countryside telling them to bring the poor, the blind, and the lame.

After they had done this, the three servants realized there was still more room so they went out through all of the land and invited everyone to the house so that it would be full.

Great Man was very pleased with this. He announced, "I tell you, not one of those people who were invited will get a taste of my banquet. But you...Eat! Eat! Have more to drink! Enjoy!"

END

Penelope's Predicament

CHARACTERS

- Narrator
- Studley Storm, our hero
- Penelope Pureheart, our heroine
- Withered N. Drawn, Penelope's maternal granny
- K-9-1-1, the rescue dog
- Couch (three sturdy males)
- Snidely Whiplash, the villain
- Mirror (a person who "reflects" everything that happens in front of him)

PROPS
Crackers

NARRATOR: This is a story of a time when men were men, and women were glad of it. Our story opens in the tiny cabin occupied by lovely Penelope Pureheart and her maternal Granny, Withered N. Drawn. Granny lay on the couch eating crackers, as Penelope did her hair in the mirror. K-9-1-1, the rescue dog, lay peacefully on the floor beside the couch, scratching fleas with his hind foot.

Yet suddenly Granny wrung her hands, and looked worried. "Penelope, dear," she said, "Studley Storm, the man of your dreams, hasn't returned from Quick Stop with our Twinkies."

Penelope flipped her hair and turned away from the mirror and said, "Don't fret, Granny—he's been gone only three weeks!" Suddenly there was a knock at the door, and K-9-1-1, the rescue dog, jumped up and barked. Penelope said, "See? That's him now!"

But who entered the cozy, tiny cabin but the evil Snidely Whiplash. He skipped to the mirror to check his moustache, while K-9-1-1 sniffed him and growled. Snidely said, "Your precious pound-cake porter won't be appearing. He popped his pinto and is presently poking up posies."

Together Penelope, Granny, and the audience screamed in horror, "What?!"

Snidely clarified: "He crashed his horse, and he's dead."

Penelope screamed. She collapsed on Granny's lap, grief-stricken. K-9-1-1, the rescue dog, ran over and licked Penelope's face.

Snidely sat down beside Penelope and stroked her hair. He said, "I'd prefer you didn't panic, my pretty. I'll pack you to the parson for a posthaste nuptial pageant."

Together Penelope, Granny, and the audience said, "What?!"

Snidely clarified, "Don't worry—you can marry me!"

K-9-1-1 barked loudly as he ran around the couch three times, barking all the way.

Just then, our hero, Studley Storm, burst into the room. He skipped to the mirror and flexed his bulbous muscles, striking several poses. He turned to Penelope and said, "This prankster has posed a profound pretense! I shall protect you from this predatory plankton!"

Together Penelope, Granny, and the audience said, "What?!"

He clarified, "I'm not really dead. I'll save you."

Snidely calmly ate a cracker as he faced off with our hero and said to him, "Perhaps you fail to perceive your perilous position, you pompous porker!"

Studley, hungry from his journey, also ate a cracker as he confronted his rival and said, "Preposterous! I shall paste you piecemeal to the pavement, you pesky poodle!"

Snidely scarfed more crackers. "Poppycock!" he said. "You perturb me. I shall pitch your puny pinhead into the potty!"

Tiring of the witty banter, our hero Studley crammed his mouth full of crackers, then said, "Pig pies! I'm provoked at your pernicious pattern of patter! I propose we punch each other in the proboscises until one of us is prostrate on the pavement."

Snidely, also fond of "Batman" reruns, replied, "Perfect!"

But then Penelope and Granny each jumped on one of the men. They pounded on their heads, screaming, "No! Don't fight! No! Don't fight!" over and over, at the top of their lungs, until they were hoarse.

Studley and Snidely finally collapsed, unconscious, to the floor.

Penelope and Granny dusted off their hands. Granny said, "Let that be a lesson to you, dearie. Violence never settled anything."

And our moral to this story is: To produce a placid and pastoral presence, practice a peaceful repudiation of the pugnacious proliferation of pain—and PARTY ON!

END

Perils of the Prodigal

A Spontaneous Melodrama

CHARACTERS

•Wise and loving father •Faithful son Larry •Flaky son Daryl •Daryl's fair-weather friends: •Lisa Luscious •Amy Airhead •Heather Hot •Henry Hunk •Pigs (at least two) •Employees (played by the friends and pigs)

Once upon a time there was a wise and loving father who had two sons, Larry and Daryl. (He used to have another son, George, but that's another story.) This wise and loving father was quite rich, owing to the fact that he was the founder of Jeans R Us at the nearby mall. (He used to own The Gap, too, but that's another store.)

The older son of this wise and loving father was a hard worker. Larry went to his father's store each day to put out new merchandise, operate the cash register, and answer the phone. The younger son of the wise and loving father, on the other hand, was spoiled. Daryl went to the store each day, too—but only to flirt with the female employees, tease his brother Larry, and "borrow" from the cash register to buy donuts at break time. But when their father came to look in on the store, Daryl started to work like crazy. Then Dad would pat both his sons on the back and exclaim, "What fine sons I have!"

One day Daryl went up to his father's office on the second floor of the mall. (His father's office used to be on the third floor, but that's another storey.) Daryl got down on his knees, clutched his father's hand, and pleaded, "Father, dearest—when you die, who will get your money?"

"I'll split it between you and Larry," replied the father. Daryl, looking earnestly into his father's eyes, said, "Can I have my half now? I want to start my own business."

The father looked like he was almost ready to cry. "I'm not sure, son," he said.

But Daryl was persistent. He wrapped himself around his father's knees and pleaded pitifully over and over again, "Please, Daddy." Finally the father agreed. He took his money and gave half to Daryl. The other half he gave to Larry.

Daryl decided to open his own Jeans R Us franchise in L.A. So he caught the next plane (**narrator throws paper** *airplane for him to catch)* to the coast. When he got there, he scratched his head and thought aloud: "There's time for work later. First I'll check out the beach." So he headed for the ocean, stopping first to pick up a new sports car *(narrator rolls a toy car for him to pick up)*. When he got to the beach, a beautiful girl came up to him. "Hi," she said, tossing her hair over her shoulder. "My name is Lisa Luscious."

Lisa took his hand, placed it around her waist, and led Daryl off to meet her friends Amy Airhead, Henry Hunk, and Heather Hot. Looking at Daryl, they all said in unison, "Hey, dude, let's party."

They all piled into Daryl's car and went cruisin'. Every day the four of them partied late into the night. Daryl bought them clothes, booze, drugs, Guns N' Roses

They were so happy that they picked Daryl up and carried him on their shoulders as they sang, to the tune of "For He's a Jolly Good Fellow," "Daryl likes to party—all the time."

One day as they were carrying Daryl around on their shoulders, he said laughingly, "Guess what guys? I'm out of money."

They dropped him like a bad habit.

Now Daryl was all alone, far from home, and broke. He lay face down on the ground and pounded it with his fists as he cried aloud, "What shall I do? What shall I do?"

Soon he found himself feeding pigs for a local farmer. The pigs were messy, and they made disgusting pig noises. Daryl paced back and forth among the swine, wondering aloud, "How could I ever have been so stupid?"

Then one day an idea hit him. He slapped his forehead so hard it knocked him backward onto one of the pigs, who made angry pig sounds at him. But that didn't bother Daryl. He picked himself up, gazed intently into the distance, and said, "I'll go back to my father. Even the stock boys in Dad's store have it better than this!" Daryl began to dance around the pig pen while the pigs squealed with delight.

The next morning Daryl got out of bed and started for home. He couldn't afford to take the plane, so he borrowed a friend's bike and pedalled feverishly. When the bike broke down, he hitch-hiked. When his ride dropped him off, he bought a used skateboard and rode it. When the bearings fell out, he began to run. Exhausted, he slowed to a walk. When the mall finally came into view, it was all he could do to crawl the last few yards to get to his father's store.

Meanwhile, his father was looking way down the length of the mall, hoping to somehow recognize his son among all the shoppers. So when he saw Daryl, he leapt for joy, let out a whoop like a banshee, and danced around in circles, jumping and clicking his heels together. Then he ran to meet his son.

Daryl wrapped himself around his father's ankles, sobbing violently while his father patted him on the head. "Father," he finally blurted out. "I am not worthy to be called your son. Make me a stock boy!"

The father took Daryl's face tenderly in his hands and lifted him to his feet. "My son is home!" he exclaimed. They embraced.

Daryl's dad took him in the store and gave him a brand new pair of Guess jeans, a pair of Air Jordans, and Oakley sunglasses. Then he invited all the employees in the store to join him and Daryl at Baskin-Robbins for ice cream. They all formed a circle around Daryl, joined hands, and danced around him singing, "For He's a Jolly Good Fellow."

But the father left the party because someone was missing—Larry. He found Larry sulking outside Baskin-Robbins, feeling sorry for himself, and sucking his thumb. As his dad approached, Larry yelled, "You don't love me! You never loved me! You always liked Daryl best! You never bought ice cream for me and

my friends!" Then he put his thumbs in his ears, stuck his tongue out at his dad, and made the ugliest face you ever saw. He was so angry he fell to the floor kicking and screaming.

The father reached down and lifted Larry to his feet. "Larry," he said "everything of mine has always been yours. But we have to be happy. My son was lost and now is found!"

Then the father and his two sons spent the next 600 years building an ark—no, wait, that's another story.

END

Two Blind Men

A Retelling of Matthew 20:29-34

CHARACTERS

•Two blind men •Two benches •Four or more people for the crowd •Jesus •Narrator
(For a larger cast, add a door, tree, rock, etc.)

Two blind men sat on benches by the roadside, humming to themselves, thinking everything was fine and dandy. One had a recurring twitch in his left hand that caused him great pain. His right arm also would jerk violently, often smacking his forehead.

The other blind man had a terrible cough. Sometimes his coughing would be replaced by a sneezing fit. He also had a strange twitch in his neck that made his head bob like a chicken's head.

A large and excited crowd following Jesus passed by the two blind men, and in the excitement people in the crowd accidentally knocked both blind men off their benches and broke the benches. The crowd moved on, leaving the coughing, twitching, and sneezing blind men in the dust. But when the two blind men heard that it was Jesus who passed by them, their coughing, twitching, and sneezing stopped. They both stood to their feet and cried out together, many times: "JOSH BEN DAVE, HAVE MERCY!"

The crowd covered their ears. They became angry with the blind men and yelled out, "Quiet! We can't hear Jesus!"

But still the blind men called out, "JOSH BEN DAVE, HAVE MERCY!"

The crowd ground their teeth and looked cross-eyed, they became so angry. They yelled, "Quiet, we said! You're too loud!" Their anger increased, and they punched and kicked the blind men, knocking them again into the dust.

But still the two moaned out, "JOSH BEN DAVE, HAVE MERCY!" The crowd became so angry, they picked up the broken pieces of the benches and threw them upon the blind men. Still the two cried out, "JOSH BEN DAVE, HAVE MERCY!"

Then Jesus came on the scene. Suddenly the crowd got a recurring twitch in their left hands that caused them great pain. Their right arms began jerking, smacking themselves in their foreheads. The crowd began coughing, some began to sneeze. All of their heads began bobbing like chickens'.

The crowd split. And Jesus healed the blind men—who then followed him offstage.

END

Sketches
With a Point

SKETCHES WITH A POINT

Not that all sketches with a serious message are themselves serious—some of these scripts wrap serious subjects in light-hearted banter and action. In any case, drama is a perfect medium for grabbing people's attention and priming them for a meeting, a talk, or a Bible study. (If you have a particular topic in mind, check out the "Topical Index to Scripts" on page 7.)

HUNG-UP ANNOUNCEMENTS

Announcement time getting stale? Try this skit. Have a piece of rope strung across the front of the room and, at the appropriate time, have a guy (dressed up like an old lady) walk in with a clothesbasket. He (she) proceeds to hang up her laundry on the clothesline, with announcements written on each article of clothing. The idea is to take the audience by total surprise. The guy should really ham it up and act like a sloppy old lady, dropping the clothes, blowing her nose on them, etc. *Steve Morgan*

THE $64,000 TESTIMONY

We all tend to use clichés when describing our faith, as this skit demonstrates (page 76). Lots of post-skit discussion possibilities here, too. *Dean Nelson*

ONE FINE DAY IN A DISASTEROUS FLOOD

Unless you are able to get hold of a 450-foot ark made out of gopher wood, the only prop you will need for this skit is a can of Coke. The script begins on page 79. *Frank Walker*

BIBLE RINGY DINGY

You don't have to be an ordained minister to have a call from God, this sketch teaches. It can be performed with few props; on the other hand, the better the props, the greater the laughs. A really drenched and dripping Jonah is immensely effective. You'll find the script on page 82.

The Operator's role is modeled after Lily Tomlin's "Ernestine the Operator" TV routines, now on video. It may help the actor who plays that part to watch the video. *Kathryn L. Zucker*

The $64,000 Testimonial

CHARACTERS
•Announcer •Buddy Bakker, host of show •Judge One •Judge Two •Judge Three •Judge Four
•3 Contestants: •Adelle Haggerty •Aunty Ruth Goldenrod •Barry Spenkowicz

ANNOUNCER: It's "The $64,000 Testimony!" And now, here's the host of "The $64,000 Testimony"...Buddy Bakker!

BUDDY BAKKER: Thank you, thank you! You're too kind! Please hold the applause! Thank you. We've got a tremendous show for you with some stiff competition! See how well you match up with our judges as we rate the testimony of our first contestant, Adelle Haggerty! Welcome to our show, Adelle. Please step up to the microphone and give us the best testimony you've got!

ADELLE HAGGERTY: Thank you, Buddy. I'd like to tell you all that Jesus is all the world to me. Life with him is joy unspeakable and full of glory, full of glory...ah, yes, full of glory, yet the half has never yet been told. Jesus never fails. What a friend I've had in Jesus since he loves me just as I am.

BUDDY BAKKER: Thank you, Adelle! Let's see how our judges respond. Judge One, on a scale of one to 10, how do you rate Ms. Haggerty?

JUDGE ONE: I gave her a four, Buddy. No new material. Disgustingly unoriginal.

BUDDY BAKKER: Thank you. Judge Two?

JUDGE TWO: I think churches are getting tired of clichés, Buddy. Sorry, but I gave her a two.

BUDDY BAKKER: Judge Three? Same answer?

JUDGE THREE: No, I put her down as average. She had a great spirit, but little content. She gets a five.

BUDDY BAKKER: And Judge Four?

JUDGE FOUR: She used nothing but outdated phrases, but at least she communicated them in a heartfelt way. I kinda liked her. I gave her an eight.

BUDDY BAKKER: Okay—how about our next contestant! Aunty Ruth Goldenrod!

AUNTY RUTH GOLDENROD: I accepted Christ when I was a child of four years, at which point I realized that my sin was making habitation for Satan. At four and one half, I was sanctified wholly, forever being cleansed of Adam's original and depraved sin. My call to the mission field did not come until I was eight years old—thus ending the three and one half years of trials and searching. I have served him unfailingly and without complaint since then. For I know my reward is in the life to come.

BUDDY BAKKER: Thank you, Aunty Ruth! Judges?

JUDGE ONE: Way beyond my attention span, Buddy. Plus she could use some zip in her delivery. I gave her a four.

JUDGE TWO: Her theology is as solid as a sponge, Buddy. She raised issues that she simply doesn't have the credentials to deal with. Sanctified at the age of four and a half? Impossible! My son is 18, and he says he still hasn't reached the age of accountability—and he <u>always</u> tells me the truth. With all that in mind, I gave Aunty Ruth a three.

BUDDY BAKKER: What about you, Judge Three?

JUDGE THREE: It was an average missionary story. I think we all could have finished her sentences for her since she had nothing new to say. I gave her a five.

BUDDY BAKKER: And Judge Four?

JUDGE FOUR: I think you're being a little tough on her when you take into account that she's in her fifties, has never married, and may be losing touch with reality. She tried hard, so I gave her an eight.

BUDDY BAKKER: I think our judges are being extra careful today! Keep in mind, you who are in our viewing audience, that this panel has heard thousands of testimonies, songs, prayers, pleas for money, and sermons. They were hand picked by me for their vast experience. They're the best in the business, if I do say so. So—you have to do something pretty zany to tickle these fellows' ears! And speaking of zany, let's bring out our third contestant, Barry Spenkowicz, who will be giving his testimony in song!

BARRY SPENKOWICZ: Life—started out

> Like a race track
>
> The starting line
>
> Covered with cars.
>
> With a word,
>
> We're all dodging and crashing,
>
> 'Till we reach the checkered flag
>
> In the stars.

BUDDY BAKKER: A creative approach indeed! Judges—how do you react? Let's start with Judge Four.

JUDGE FOUR: His vibrato was good and singing without accompaniment like that takes guts and perfect pitch. I gave him a seven.

BUDDY BAKKER: Okay, Judge Three?

JUDGE THREE: It sounds to me like he could use a tune up—ho! ho! Seriously, though, the song had good emotional appeal but little eternal value. I gave him a six for his musical ability.

BUDDY BAKKER: And Judge Two.

JUDGE TWO: The song was fine but he really tried to force his personality on us. A real cheesy smile, you know. For that I gave him a one.

BUDDY BAKKER: Judge One?

JUDGE ONE: Analogies are outdated, Buddy. That made it just under average, so I gave him a four.

BUDDY BAKKER: Well, that's it for tonight. Our judges are tabulating the scores to see who our big winner is. The winner is...Oh! I can't believe it...the winner is Aunty Ruth Goldenrod! Congratulations, Aunty Ruth Goldenrod, you have won the $64,000 Testimony!

AUNTY RUTH GOLDENROD: Oh! Oh! Oh! I am so excited! Oh, praise the Lord! Oh, I'm so happy and here's the reason why!

BUDDY BAKKER: And what is the reason, Aunty?

AUNTY RUTH GOLDENROD: What?

BUDDY BAKKER: I say, what is the reason you're so happy?

AUNTY RUTH GOLDENROD: I don't know what you're talking about, smarty pants.

BUDDY BAKKER: But, Aunty Ruth Goldenrod, you just said, "I'm so happy and here's the reason why." So why are you so happy?

AUNTY RUTH GOLDENROD: What are you? An intellectual or something? How do I know why. I just said it...I don't have to answer your tricky questions.

BUDDY BAKKER: Well. That's all the time we have, folks. Tonight's big winner of "The $64,000 Testimony" has been Aunty Ruth Goldenrod. Tune in again next week when we'll have three new contestants with three old testimonies that could just be the $64,000 Testimony!

END

ONE FINE DAY IN A DISASTROUS

FLOOD

CHARACTERS
•Noah •His son Ham

• •

Noah and Ham walk onstage; both rock back and forth as though they are in a boat. Ham looks sick.

HAM: *(groans)* Ohhhhh...

NOAH: What seems to be the trouble, Ham my boy?

HAM: I don't feel so good.

NOAH: You don't look so good either. What seems to be the problem?

HAM: It stinks in here. These animals smell worse than a dead skunk in a heat wave.

NOAH: Oh, come now. It can't be all that bad, just because we have two of every animal in the world in this ark.

HAM: Well, that's not all. This boat is rocking back and forth and back and forth. We've been in here 326 days, 12 hours, three minutes, and 17 seconds. We've been floating in this water for so long I'm starting to feel like a tea bag.

NOAH: Hey, don't worry son. I don't think God is going to keep us in here too much longer. You must have patience.

HAM: Maybe for another 49 days, 11 hours, and possibly 57 minutes, and 43 seconds—counting leap year—don't you think?

NOAH: Yes, maybe...

HAM: Using math-o-matics of course.

NOAH: Quite right, but you know you must learn to be patient, patient, patient, patient...

HAM: Dad, Dad, Dad—you're starting to sound like a doctor.

NOAH: I'm sorry. Is it still raining outside?

HAM: Does it ever rain on the inside?

NOAH: No respect, no respect.

HAM: Take a peek and see.

NOAH: *(looks out window)* It's raining so hard I can't see what the weather's like.

HAM: Let me see, Dad. *(looks out window)* Why, it's raining cats and dogs outside.

NOAH: Son, I told you to keep those animals inside the ark.

HAM: That was only a figure of speech. It sure rains a lot.

NOAH: Yes son, I think we're over the future site of Seattle, Washington. That reminds me, I think I left the water running in the bathtub back home.

HAM: Uh oh, Dad. When we get the water bill, Mom's going to kill you!

NOAH: I hope you meant that as a figure of speech.

HAM: Hey Dad, do boats sink often?

NOAH: Only once.

HAM: What if we get a hole in the ark and it sinks?

NOAH: Impossible. For one thing, God wouldn't allow us to sink; that would ruin the whole story. Besides, I can't swim.

HAM: What if we did sink? We don't have any life preservers big enough to fit the elephants.

NOAH: Oh, you're such a ham, Ham. Trust God. He's holding this boat together just as he holds our lives together. He will safely float you through any flood waters of life if you just put your trust in him and let him be your captain.

HAM: But things are just so dull around here. I wake up in the morning to the rooster's crow, to the pig's oink, and to the zebras...whatever noise they make. Have you ever tried to get a 600-pound Siberian tiger to use a litter box? Don't. Also Dad, you've got to do something with those dive-bombing birds. I have to wash my hair every hour because of them. Speaking of which, have you seen my hair dryer lying around the ark?

NOAH: Yes, I have. While I was drying my beard with it, the ostrich swallowed it; shocking sight.

HAM: You're kidding. I don't know how much more of this I can handle.

NOAH: What, this ark?

HAM: No, your jokes.

NOAH: Like I said before, you must have patience.

HAM: Oh, I have patience. I've always had patience. Ever since I was born I've had patience. *(pause)* What's patience?

NOAH: Patience is the suffering of affliction with a calm, unruffled temper. When you're patient through times of trial and tribulation, God will shape and mold you into a new and better you.

HAM: But Dad, I'm so bored. This whole place is totally boring. I want off this ark.

NOAH: But son, don't you want to grow?

HAM: What do you mean? Does being bored help me to grow? That's totally wild; I suppose if I was excited it would stunt my growth.

NOAH: No son, I don't mean that kind of growth. I'm talking about your spiritual growth. You see, through each trial and tribulation we should praise God because we can benefit spiritually and grow to be a stronger Christian for God.

HAM: I see, we should rejoice in our sufferings because we know that suffering produces patience, patience produces character, and character produces hope.

NOAH: Exactly son. We benefit from our boredom. So just be patient until...until the great rainbow in the sky shines bright.

HAM: Thanks Dad. I'll finish cleaning out the stalls.

NOAH: Hurry up, Mom's cooking dinner.

HAM: What are we having?

NOAH: What do you want?

HAM: Barbecue barley with cheese sauce.

NOAH: Want a side order of fries with that?

HAM: No thanks, maybe some alfalfa sprouts topped with ketchup.

NOAH: You've got it.

HAM: Oh, by the way Dad, have you seen any sight of dry land yet?

NOAH: I sent out a raven earlier this morning to find dry land, but that raven had aquatic phobia. *(to the audience)* That's the fear of water. With the water below him and the rain around him, that bird freaked.

HAM: Why don't we try it again, only with a smaller animal.

NOAH: I know, I'll use a snake.

HAM: Naaa, Harold's got a cold. Besides, that snake is so nearsighted he fell deeply in love with a rope.

NOAH: I bet his love life is all tied up.

HAM: Why don't we use a dove?

NOAH: Naaa, that won't work. *(pause)* I know, we'll use a dove.

HAM: *(to himself)* Why didn't I think of that?

NOAH: Here pretty bird. *(Noah acts as if he were reaching into a cage for a dove)* Now listen carefully, I want you to fly out and find dry ground, and if you do find dry ground, bring something back as proof. Good luck and God be with you. *(throws the dove out the window)* Fly and be free. *(mime watching the bird fly, then fall down into the water)* Swim, swim, flap your wings like this. *(flap arms)* That's it, go, go, go. *(to son)* Remind me to sign up that bird for the next Olympics.

HAM: Right.

NOAH: Look.

HAM: Where?

NOAH: Up there, the dove returns, and it has something in its beak. *(a can of Coke is thrown onstage, Noah catches it)* Look, the dove has found land.

HAM: *(grabs the Coke can and holds it out to the audience)* It's the real thing.

NOAH: *(Noah sings part of the Coke jingle)* Coca-Cola...oh, anyway, I knew God wouldn't let us down, you just got to have...

HAM: I know, I know, have a little patience.

NOAH: You've got it now, my boy. Oh no!

HAM: What?

NOAH: I just thought of something.

HAM: What?

NOAH: Oh no!

HAM: What!?

NOAH: I hope we can find a hotel with a vacant room.

HAM: Don't worry, I bet a lot of people stayed home because of the rain.

(they exit)

END

Bible Ringy Dingy

CHARACTERS

•Operator •Moses •Jonah •Sarah •Everyman/Everywoman

A paper-covered desk sits stage right, where a telephone operator—à la Lily Tomlin's "Ernestine the Operator"— works, her back to stage left, where all the other characters enter and speak from.

OPERATOR: One ringy dingy, two ringy—oh! Gracious good evening, and hello. Is this the party to whom I am speaking? Ah yes, is a Moses there please...what?...*(loud laugh and snort)* I'm sorry. I misunderstood. May I please be speaking to him? Thank you.

MOSES: *(enters shakily, verging on stuttering voice, obviously worried and anxious that there's a call for him)* Hello?

OPERATOR: Um, yes. Is this a Mr. Moses?

MOSES: Yeah, is there a problem?

OPERATOR: *(snorting)* Oh! Mr. Moses you're so funny. Now, Mr. Moses, it says in my file that you are being called to request a transfer from a Mr. Pharaoh of Egypt. Is this information correct?

MOSES: Uhhh...well...I...uhhh...

OPERATOR: Please Mr. Moses. There's no use hedging...or should I say no "burning bushing"? *(big guffaw and snort)*

MOSES: Please. I've already discussed this with God. I thought he decided to give my brother Aaron a call instead.

OPERATOR: I beg to differ. Our records clearly show that although your brother may assist in operations, this is not a conference call. God has clearly chosen you.

MOSES: *(big sigh)* I have no problems having a relationship with God. I just don't want him calling me all the time. Don't you have call blocking available or something?

OPERATOR: Oh Mr. Moses, I'm sorry that's not possible. Having a relationship with God means that, for starters, you at least listen when he calls. I'm sure God will help you, but you need to return his call.

MOSES: Well...will God help with the charges?

OPERATOR: Of course.

MOSES: God will be with me?

OPERATOR: Every step of the way.

MOSES: Okay, I'll return God's call.

(exits stage left)

JONAH: *(enters, soaking wet, shivering, miserable; he speaks this line with a Brooklyn accent, mocking the classic operator line)* Hello! Is this the party to whom I am speaking?

OPERATOR: This is she. May I help you?

JONAH: Yeah, this is Jonah! I need to talk to my travel agent and I want to talk to him now!

OPERATOR: One moment please...*(pause)* Oh, you're <u>that</u> Jonah.

JONAH: *(yelling)* What was your first clue?!

OPERATOR: *(giggling)* Oh, Mr. Jonah, we've been expecting to hear from you! Have you found your accommodations to be less than to your liking?

JONAH: I'm in a whale! Have you ever smelled the inside of a whale?

OPERATOR: Oh, gracious no, but then I didn't try to reverse the charges on my call either.

JONAH: What are you talking about?

OPERATOR: Oh, Mr. Jonah, our records clearly show that you were called to go to Nineveh and you refused to accept charges. Did you really think you could get away with this, Mr. Jonah? Did you not realize we are omnipotent here? That's "potent" with an "omni." *(snorts)*

JONAH: So you're saying I can't reverse the charges? I have to accept the call that I got?

OPERATOR: Now you have it, Mr. Jonah.

JONAH: Will God be with me?

OPERATOR: Every step of the way.

JONAH: Well, fine. Okay. Thank you. I guess... *(exits stage left, Sarah enters)*

OPERATOR: Gracious good day and hello. Is this the party to whom I am speaking?

SARAH: This is Sarah, yes. Can I help you?

OPERATOR: Yes, this is the telephone company calling. I have a requisition form from a Sarai, Abram's wife. Something about a three-way calling hookup gone wrong.

SARAH: Oh yes, I'm Sarah!

OPERATOR: This form says I'm looking for Sarah.

SARAH: Yes, well, both my husband's name and mine were changed just recently...*(sweet sarcasm)* I figured since the telephone company is omniscient you would already know that.

OPERATOR: We knew. I was just making sure you had accepted this change. You seemed to be having trouble lately accepting the call God has on your life.

SARAH: Well, we originally had a three-way calling arrangement between myself, my husband, and...ah...a servant whom I had reason to dislike.

OPERATOR: *(big snort and giggle)* Oh yes! We're still talking about that one up here! But I was under the impression that this situation had been taken care of.

SARAH: Well, it has. But while I have you on the phone...is it true that I am going to give birth to a son?

OPERATOR: Promise you won't laugh?

SARAH: *(looking down, a bit ashamed)* I promise.

OPERATOR: You have been called to give birth to a son named Isaac.

SARAH: *(excitedly)* Oh! Thank you! *(exits stage left)*

EVERYMAN: *(enters irritably, having been interrupted in his work by this call; picks up the phone, answers gruffly)* Hello!

OPERATOR: *(for the first time is taken aback)* Ummmm...uhh...oh yes! Gracious good day and...aaah! Is this the party to whom I am speaking?

EVERYMAN: Yeah! I'm busy! Whaddaya want?

OPERATOR: Oh! Pardon me, sir, for interrupting, but there is a call for you on line three.

EVERYMAN: Three? Whaddaya mean three? We only have two lines!

83

OPERATOR: Oh sir! But this is a direct line! You have a call to ministry from God.

EVERYMAN: What are you talking about? I already have a job. I work as a repairman. *(moves to slam phone down, but the Operator's next words stop him just in time)*

OPERATOR: Oh sir, wait! I beg to differ. God wants you to understand your ministry is as a repairman. You are using your gifts given to you by God in the world. It's your special calling.

EVERYMAN: You mean I'm in ministry? Well, I never thought I'd...I mean...God is calling me? But I'm not good with people. There are other people more religious than me around. Call them! Get them to do it! And oh yeah—*(relieved that he's just thought of another excuse)*—I don't have time to think about anything else.

OPERATOR: Oh gracious sir! *(snort)* Very impressive. You were able to get in all the top excuses in

one breath. This cuts down considerably on time. No wonder you're so successful. Your people skills are needed in this world. You can show people what a Christian life is like.

EVERYMAN: So do I have a choice?

OPERATOR: Well, we like to say you do, but we usually get our people in the end...one way or the other.

EVERYMAN: Oh, all right then. Fine, I'll do it! But will God help me and be with me?

OPERATOR: God will always be with you! And, sir—

EVERYMAN: *(starts to leave, but he turns around for final message)* Yes?

OPERATOR: Thank you for accepting God's call.

END

WHY IS LIFE SO EMPTY?

This easy-to-prepare sketch (page 86) will get your youths thinking about the emptiness of many of their favorite ways to spend time. *Jay Ashcraft*

THE TIME IS RIGHT

The sketch that begins on page 88 gets your junior high students thinking about Jesus. *Jay Ashcraft*

TEN PERCENT

Introduce the topic of tithing with this sketch. Afterward use questions like these to explore the subject:
• After hearing what Emily's dad said about tithing, if you were Emily, would you give $2 to the church? Why or why not?
• Why do you think God is interested in your money? Are there other things you can tithe besides cash?
• Do you know how our church spends the tithes and offerings it collects? (Be prepared to answer this question knowledgeably if you're going to ask it.)
• (First read Leviticus 27:30-32, Psalm 96:7-8, and Mark 12:17—all of which deal with tithing.) According to these verses, why should a Christian tithe?
• What do these verses tell us about the character of God—that is, about who God is and what he wants from his people?
• Are the good things in your life directly from God, the result of hard work, or the result of chance?
• Why might a person actually enjoy tithing?

It's Saturday afternoon. Emily has just walked in the door from a baby-sitting job. Her dad is in the den watching a football game.

EMILY: Dad, look! I just made 20 bucks baby-sitting for the Henrys! Will you take me to the mall? Please?

DAD: We'll see. *(looks up from TV)* Are you saving two dollars for your tithe tomorrow?

EMILY: I can't tomorrow. I need it all for Christmas presents. Do you know how many friends I have to get presents for besides you and mom and Chrissy? Besides, I earned it. It's my money.

DAD: *(slowly)* Yes. It is your money. Ninety percent of it is, anyway. The first 10 percent belongs to God. It's what God has always required of his followers.

EMILY: Yeah. I know you and mom tithe. But I don't make that much money. It just doesn't seem fair to have to give 10 percent to the church.

DAD: Sometimes 10 percent really does seem like a lot. But you know, Em, ever since your mom and I made the commitment to tithe, we've never come up short financially. Sure, it's tight sometimes—you know that—but God has always provided enough. And in some amazing ways, too.

EMILY: Can we go to the mall now?

DAD: Hang on. This is important stuff. As you decide whether or not to give God two dollars tomorrow, I think it's important to consider the fact that it's God who gave you the ability to be a good baby-sitter, and that it's God who's provided you a good job with the Henrys. God is looking after you, Em, and he expects you to honor him with that 10 percent. Will you think about these things before you make your decision to spend all the money?

EMILY: I'll try, Dad. I really will. *(pause)* Can we go to the mall now? *Anne Elizabeth Dodge Tyson*

JESUS MET A WOMAN

Scripture readings come alive when the text is prepared in script form. Many of the narrative sections of both Old and New Testaments may be adapted for group use with excellent results. Assign parts, have a reading, and then discuss the content of the play. Follow up with discussion questions shown below:
• Discuss the woman's growing conception of who Jesus was. Who do you think Jesus was?
• Compare and contrast Jesus' attitude, the disciples' attitude, and the typical Jewish attitude toward this woman of another race.
• What is the living water of which Jesus spoke?
• What did Jesus teach the woman about worship?
• Discuss the nature of the harvest Jesus spoke about.
• If you took the teachings of this passage seriously, what specific differences could there be in your life tomorrow?

Jesus' conversation with the Samaritan woman is on page 91. *William Chaney*

WHY IS LIFE SO
EMPTY?

CHARACTERS
•Amy •Lisa •Salesman •Ree Ality

PROPS
•Large glass of milk •Balloon marked BOYFRIEND •Balloon marked SPORTS •Balloon marked FANTASY •Large pin •Pillows or sofa

---

Amy and Lisa are lounging on pillows or a sofa.

AMY: Life is so boring. It seems like nothing I do really means anything. I feel like a zit on the face of life.

LISA: Listen, Amy. I know what you mean, but maybe you should try what I do. I'm drinking milk. My life may be a dud now, but in a few years...if I keep drinking milk, everything will be great.

AMY: Yeah, right. *(Salesman knocks at the door)*

LISA: Get the door, Amy. Maybe it's some guys.

AMY: *(opens the door)* Yes?

SALESMAN: I understand your life is boring.

AMY: How'd you know?

SALESMAN: I have my ways. Listen, I have some things in this bag that are guaranteed to give your life purpose and meaning.

AMY: I don't think so...

SALESMAN: Don't be so sure. Look, here's a real hot item. I've been selling lots of these lately. *(pulls out a balloon with BOYFRIEND written on it)*

LISA: Like, what is it?

SALESMAN: The promise of a boyfriend. As soon as you get one of these, your life will be worth living. Everything will fall into place once you have a boyfriend.

AMY: *(grabs the balloon)* I'll take it!

SALESMAN: Hey, relax. I've got lots more really good stuff. Take this item for example. *(pulls out another balloon with SPORTS on it)*

LISA: Whoa, cool! What is it?

SALESMAN: This baby is running a real close second to boys. If you become a jock, you'll never feel like something's missing again.

LISA: Wicked, dude! *(grabs the balloon)* I'll take it. Like, this is totally rad.

SALESMAN: Well, I've got to run. But since you're such good customers, I'll give you each a special bonus.

LISA: Like, unbelievable, dude! What is it?

SALESMAN: I call this little baby "Emergency Happiness." Just in case, for some unexplainable reason, boys or sports aren't enough, just pull this priceless beauty out, and bingo!—all your problems are solved. It's called Fantasy. *(pulls out balloon with the word FANTASY on it)*

AMY: How do you use that?

SALESMAN: Easy. Any time you're bored, go into a fantasy world. Music can do it, so can movies. Anything, in fact, that keeps your mind off what your life is really like. Some of my best customers use fantasy almost 24 hours a day. They even go to sleep with Walkmans on at night, and wake up with them in the morning.

AMY: Well, what's this all gonna cost us?

SALESMAN: Don't worry. Payment is painless—you simply pay me in hundreds of easy installments. Just give me a week of your life here, a day there. You'd be surprised how the hours add up.

AMY: Great, we'll each take one.

SALESMAN: Now remember, if for some reason these items don't do the job, I've got plenty of other great ideas where these came from. *(exits)*

LISA: Hey, this is unbelievable. This guy shows up just when we need him the most. We've got some great stuff here. Like, I just can't wait to start using it. *(Ree Ality knocks at the door)*

AMY: Now what? *(answers the door)*

REE ALITY: Good evening ladies. Ality's my name. Ree Ality. I hear you recently purchased some new toys to keep life interesting.

AMY: How'd you know?

REE ALITY: I have my ways. Now let's take a look at what you've got.

LISA: Sure! Check this out. Isn't it, like, totally awesome? *(holds up her SPORTS balloon)*

REE ALITY: Sports, eh? That's nice—but what happens when you get injured or don't make the team? Or what if you win everything? What have you really got to show for it that's worthwhile and satisfying? No, I'm afraid that sports just doesn't cut it. *(he pulls out a pin and pops her balloon)*

LISA: Hey! Look what you did to my sports!

REE ALITY: That's life.

AMY: Well, what about this? *(she holds up her BOYFRIEND balloon)*

REE ALITY: That still doesn't cut it. What about when some boy dumps you or uses you? What about when you finally get the hunk of your dreams and he turns out to be boring? Worse, what if he turns out to be everything you've always wanted and he's still not perfect? No. I'm afraid that one has to go, too. *(she tries to pull back her balloon, but he pops it anyway)*

AMY: Hey, that really hurt. Why don't you just get out of here? And don't come back!

REE ALITY: Don't worry, I'll be back. *(leaves)*

LISA: Man, what a bummer. That guy was a real loser.

AMY: Yeah, it's a good thing he didn't see our fantasies. He would have popped those, too.

LISA: Amy, I think we need to go find the man with the balloons. Fantasies aren't enough to keep me going all the time.

AMY: Just keep drinking your milk, Lisa.

END

The TimE Is RigHt

CHARACTERS
•Arch Angel, the game show host •Haley, first contestant •Jessie, second contestant
•Zoe, third contestant •Cue card holder •Delivery person

PROPS

- Small jewelry box, with a note inside
- Bag, with a note inside
- 3 Cue cards:—OHHHH, with a sad face
  —AHHHH, with a sad face
  —APPLAUSE AND CHEERS, with a happy face
- Official-looking document in an envelope
- 3 Large gift-wrapped boxes, each with a note inside:
  —one box marked GOD'S KINGDOM
  —one marked SATISFACTION GUARANTEED
  —one marked PAID IN FULL

Stage or room front looks like a game show. The Cue card holder not only holds up the cue cards at the appropriate moments, but also elicits responses from the audience.

ARCH ANGEL: Welcome to "The Time Is Right!" And now let's meet our contestants. Haley Williams! Come on down! Jessie Erickson! Come on down! Zoe Roberts! Come on down! *(contestants jump up from their seats in the audience and run screaming to the stage)* Now contestants, you know how the game goes. Each of you has something that you hope to get out of life. You will all have the choice to trade that hope in for one of God's fabulous gifts, or to hang on to it and see if it turns out like you planned. All right. Let's start with contestant Number One. Haley, what do you have there with you?

HALEY: *(holds up jewelry box)* I'm hoping that I will become a successful model. That will make me happy.

ARCH ANGEL: Haley, box number one is marked GOD'S KINGDOM. Would you like to trade in your box for this fabulous gift from God, or would you prefer to hang on to what you've got?

HALEY: I think I'll take my chances with what I've got.

ARCH ANGEL: Haley, are you sure?

HALEY: I'm sure.

ARCH ANGEL: Okay, Haley. Let's see what you missed. *(opens the box marked GOD'S KINGDOM; he pulls out a note)* Let's see what it says. "Delight yourself in the Lord and he will give you the desires of your heart."

CUE CARD: *(OHHHH with a sad face)*

ARCH ANGEL: That's too bad, Haley. But let's see what you ended up with.

HALEY: *(opens the jewelry box and read the note inside)* "Disappointment, heartache, regret." *(Haley starts to sob)*

CUE CARD: *(AHHHH with a sad face)*

ARCH ANGEL: I'd say, "Better luck next time Haley," but on this show you only get one chance. Goodbye...and don't forget to take your future with you. *(Haley leaves dejectedly)* Contestant Number Two, Jessie Erickson, what have you got there with you?

JESSIE: Nothing. I don't have anything. I figure that if I don't expect anything out of life I won't be disappointed.

ARCH ANGEL: But surely you must have something.

JESSIE: Nope. I just take life as it comes.

ARCH ANGEL: All right then, Jessie. Would you like to trade what you have for what's inside box number two? God's fabulous gift is labeled SATISFACTION GUARANTEED.

JESSIE: No. Like I said, I would rather not expect anything. Then I won't be disappointed.

ARCH ANGEL: Okay, Jessie. You expect nothing. So let's see what you receive.

DELIVERY PERSON: Special delivery for Jessie Erickson. *(hands Jessie an envelope)*

ARCH ANGEL: Go ahead, Jessie. Read what it says.

JESSIE: "Jessie Erickson, you are hereby summoned to appear before The Most Supreme Court where the Creator of the Universe will pronounce his judgment." What a rip-off! I thought that if I just let life happen, everything would turn out fine!

ARCH ANGEL: Sounds like a big mistake, Jessie. Now let's see what you missed. *(opens present labeled SATISFACTION GUARANTEED)* Look at this! A promise from God: "I will never leave you or turn my back on you."

CUE CARD: *(AHHHH with a sad face)*

ARCH ANGEL: Goodbye Jessie. Don't forget to take your summons with you. And now for our final contestant. Zoe Roberts, what have you brought with you?

ZOE: *(holds up bag)* Well, it's kind of a mixed bag. I put in all the good things and bad things I've done. I'm hoping the good things outweigh the bad.

ARCH ANGEL: Zoe, now it's time for the big decision. Do you want to keep what you have or take box number three, God's fabulous gift marked PAID IN FULL?

ZOE: Well, I've been watching very carefully and I think I have a better chance taking what God has to offer than doing it my way. I'll take God's gift.

ARCH ANGEL: Zoe, go ahead and open your bag. Let's see what you missed.

ZOE: Boy, I'm glad I didn't get this. "If anyone does everything right yet breaks one of the commandments, that person is guilty of breaking them all."

CUE CARD: *(OHHHH with a sad face)*

ARCH ANGEL: And now, let's see what you receive. *(opens up the box)* It says, "Life that just keeps going and going and going."

CUE CARD: *(APPLAUSE AND CHEERS with a happy face)*

ZOE: *(jumping up and down)* What a great gift!

ARCH ANGEL: Congratulations, Zoe! You're our grand prize winner today! *(turns to the audience)* And remember to tune in next time, because it might be your *(points to the audience)* turn to play "The Time Is Right."

END

Jesus Met a Woman

CHARACTERS
•Narrator •Jesus •Woman •Disciple

BIBLE TEXT
John 4

NARRATOR: Jesus was journeying northward from Judea to Galilee and he had to pass through Samaria on the way. It was located near the village of Sychar on the piece of property that Jacob had given to his son, Joseph. Tired from the long walk in the hot sun, Jesus sat down beside a well while his disciples went into the village to buy food. A Samaritan woman came to the well to draw water.

JESUS: Would you give me a drink of water?

WOMAN: You are a Jew and I am a Samaritan—how can you ask me for a drink?

NARRATOR: The Jews usually would not even speak to Samaritans, much less drink from the same cup.

JESUS: If you only knew what a wonderful gift God could give you and who I am, you would ask me for some living water.

WOMAN: But you don't even have a bucket and this is a deep well. Where would you get living water? Besides, you surely are not greater than our ancestor, Jacob. How can you offer better water than this which he and his family and his cattle drank?

JESUS: Everyone who drinks the water from this well will become thirsty again, but whoever drinks the water I will give him will never be thirsty again. For my gift will become a spring within him which will provide him with living water and give him eternal life.

WOMAN: Please sir—give me some of that water! Then I'll never be thirsty again and won't have to make this long trip out here to draw water.

JESUS: Go, get your husband, and then come back here.

WOMAN: But, I'm not married.

JESUS: You are telling the truth when you say you are not married. You have been married to five men, and the man you are living with now is not really your husband.

WOMAN: You must be a prophet, sir! But, if I may ask a question: Why do you Jews insist that Jerusalem is the only place of worship? We Samaritans, meanwhile, claim it is where our ancestors worshipped—here at Mount Gerizim.

JESUS: Believe me, ma'am, the time is coming when we will no longer be concerned about the place to worship the Father! For it's not where we worship that's important, but how we worship. Worship must be spiritual and real, for God is Spirit and we must have his Spirit's help to worship as we should. The Father wants this kind of worship. But you Samaritans know so little about him, worshipping with your eyes shut, so to speak. We Jews know all about him, for salvation comes to mankind through the Jewish race.

WOMAN: Well, at least I know that the Messiah will come—you know, the one they call Christ—and when he does, he will make everything plain to us.

JESUS: I am the Messiah!

NARRATOR: Then the woman left her water pot beside the well, went back to the village, and excitedly told everyone about Jesus. Soon the people came streaming from the village to see him. In the meantime, the disciples had returned to Jesus. They had seen him talking to the Samaritan woman and were astonished, but they did not ask Jesus why nor what he had said to the woman. Instead they urged Jesus to eat.

DISCIPLE: Teacher, eat some of the food we bought.

JESUS: No. I have some food you don't know about.

DISCIPLE: *(to other disciples)* Did someone else bring him food?

JESUS: My nourishment comes from doing the will of God who sent me and from finishing his work. Do you think the work of harvesting will not begin until the summer ends—four months from now? Open your eyes and look around you! Fields of human souls are ripening all around us and they are ready for harvesting. The reaper of the harvest is being paid now and he gathers the crops for eternal life; the planter and the reaper will be glad together, for in this harvest the old saying comes true: "One man plants and another reaps." I have sent you to harvest a crop in a field where you did not labor; others labored there and you profit from their work.

NARRATOR: Many of the Samaritans in that town believed in Jesus because the Woman had told them of his ability to know all things. So when the Samaritans came to him, they begged him to stay with them and Jesus stayed there two days. Many more believed because of Jesus' own words, and the villagers told the woman: "We believe now, not because of what you said, but because we have heard him with our own ears, and we know that he is the Savior of the world."

END

TOM MEETS GOD

Turn to page 94 for a skit with a message (that should be well-rehearsed before presenting to the group). Follow up the skit with a discussion of what happened. Although this skit is quite short, there are several issues raised worth getting into.
Abiding Savior Lutheran Church

SACRIFICE? ME? YOU GOTTA BE KIDDING!

As the simple, no-prop skit for two on page 95 demonstrates, you can use light drama—read or memorized—to interpret or present a Scripture passage to your group. This skit is based on Romans 12:1-2. Write similar skits on other passages you'll be teaching—or let your kids write their own as part of a Bible study. *Myra Shofner*

TALK TO ME!

This four-scene sketch (page 97) demonstrates four levels of communication people commonly use to relate to one another: superficial, gossip, opinion, and feeling. Use the scenes to introduce a discussion about the games people play in their communication with others.

Reference the context of the audience. For example, if you're performing these during a retreat, have the Liz character tell her feelings about the weekend (this is, in fact, how this script is written—adapt it to fit your situation). Then let the Chrissy and Sharon characters respond in kind. And Liz's final line in scene four should ask how the audience feels about the youth group, or the mission trip, or the church, or whatever. Follow up with a discussion about the importance of honesty and openness in communication in order to grow healthy friendships.

Want to make it more personal? Replace the script names of the actors with their actual names. *Frank Zolvinski*

MISSIONS MICROCOSM

You can dramatize the need for world missions with this skit, which the youths can present themselves to an entire congregation with effective results.

While the dialogue (on page 100—adapt it to fit your own church's missions situation) is going on in the front of the room, other young people are circulating throughout the congregation, pretending to proselyte for converts. The following "missionaries" can mingle throughout the room (let the listed number of each kind of missionary suggest the proportion more than the actual number):

• **1 Christian,** who can say something like this: "I'm a Christian because I do my best to follow Jesus Christ. Of course God doesn't want anyone to miss him, but many in the world are lost because they do not know Jesus. Can you help me tell them?"

• **2 Hindus** can say something like "As Hindus, we worship many gods and reverence many animals, who may be our reincarnated ancestors. With great moral effort, and with several lives on this earth, one can eventually transcend the cycle of birth, death, and reincarnation—and finally reach nirvana."

• **3 Moslems:** "There is one God, and his name is Allah. Mohammed is his prophet. Allah requires moral purity in his children—no contamination by the world's evil influences. The Koran is to be studied, for it tells us how to live righteous lives."

• **3 Buddhists:** "Don't you want to live a peaceful and tranquil life? Quiet contemplation can begin in the center of your being and, with discipline and practice, flood your body, your mind, your soul with peace, with insight, with calm certainty."

• **1 member of the American Humanist Society:** "Who has time for an insecure bully like the Old Testament Jehovah or a misdirected peasant that the first century Romans martyred on a cross? Trust yourself, not religious mythmakers—who are responsible for most of the greed and misery in the world."

• **4 animists—that is, worshippers of many spirits in nature:** "We must worship the living things we see around us, or else they will turn against us in their anger and kill us and our children. So we feed these spirits and sacrifice to them."

All these should move quietly throughout the congregation, distributing their religious literature, briefly stating their dogma (as summarized above), and asking people if they would like to follow Buddha, or Allah, or the sun, etc.

When the speakers on the platform have finished, the world "missionaries" all come to the front, stand in a line, and introduce themselves with a final repetition of their dogma (above). Then explain to the congregation that the number of these "missionaries" are roughly proportionate to the religions they were propogating. Christians are actually outnumbered 14 to one. *David Farnum*

Tom Meets God

CHARACTERS
•Tom •Angel •God

TOM: *(knocks and Angel opens the door)* Hi! My name is Tom. I would like to see the person in charge, please.

ANGEL: Sure, come on in.

TOM: Look, uh, I know this guy is really important, but do you think he would see someone like me?

ANGEL: He sees everyone. You can see him any time you'd like.

TOM: Could I see him now?

ANGEL: Go right on in.

TOM: Now?

ANGEL: Yes.

TOM: *(hesitates and then slowly walks in)* Uh, excuse me, my name is Tom. I wondered if I could see you for a few minutes?

GOD: I've got all the time you need.

TOM: Well, I'm going to high school right now, and I am a little confused about what I should do. A couple of my friends say you can help, but they seem just as confused as I am. To be quite honest, I haven't really been impressed by your work. I mean, don't get me wrong, my friends are really good friends, you know, and they really seem to like me, but, they haven't got it so good. Bob, one of my friends, has a dad that is an alcoholic and my other friend's folks are getting a divorce. The crazy thing is my folks are great, I really love them, everything's going great...except...except I can't seem to see the point in life. In spite of all the junk that is happening to my friends, they really seem to be convinced that you are important. So that's why I'm here. I just thought you could give me some pointers. I just feel kinda lost.

GOD: My price is kind of high.

TOM: That's okay, because my folks are pretty well off. What is it?

GOD: All.

TOM: All?

GOD: Yes, all. Everything.

TOM: Sheesh. Don't you have a layaway plan? How about a pay as you go? Isn't your profit margin a little out of line?

GOD: Actually, my cost was quite high. Ask my Son.

TOM: Well, uh, I think I'll have to wait a while. I appreciate you're taking the time to talk to me and I'm sure you're worth it, it's just that at my age, it's a little too soon to give up everything. After all, when you're young that's when the good times happen. Besides, I think I can get what I'm looking for at a much cheaper price.

GOD: Be careful, Tom. The price you pay up front may be cheaper, but your cost in the long run may be much higher than you ever anticipated.

TOM: Yeah, sure. Well, nice talking to you, God. Maybe I'll see you around some time.

GOD: There's no maybe about it. See you soon, Tom.

END

x

Sacrifice? Me? You Gotta Be Kidding!

An Interpretation of Romans 12:1-2, for 2 characters

1: I beg you, Christians, because God is so merciful, present your bodies as living sacrifices—holy and acceptable to God. This is the reasonable way to serve God.

2: Sacrifice! Sacrifice? When you say sacrifice, I think of some pagan tribe in Africa, and a living body lying on a rock slab, with fire under the slab and the body burning as a sacrifice to an idol. You want me to be a sacrifice? No thanks. I'm too young to die.

1: Who said anything about dying? God wants you alive—a living sacrifice—which means to live for God—serving and loving him.

2: Oh. That sounds a little better. *(pause)* But I don't know. It sounds like I'd have to give up a lot. I mean I really enjoy living—doing the things I want to do. You know what I mean?

1: Yes, I know what you mean. But being a living sacrifice means a change of mind—you no longer want to do what you want to do—instead you want to do what God wants you to do.

2: Wanting to do what God wants me to do instead of wanting to do what I want to do? That sounds like a lot of double-talk. *(pause)* Besides I already don't really want to do what I want to do. Mostly I want to do what my friends want to do.

1: Conformity?

2: Huh?

1: You are talking about conformity, aren't you? Your mind is set on conforming to the world's standards. Is that right?

2: Yes, that's right. Uh? I mean, no, that's not right is it? I mean...it's what I mean, but it's not right.

1: So you do know the difference?

2: Of course. I am a Christian. I know the Bible says "Be not conformed to this world." But it's very difficult not to be. You know what I mean?

1: Sure, I have the same problem.

2: You do?

1: All Christians do. The pull of the world is very strong. Everything and everybody encourages us to conform. That is—everybody but God who made us. He knows us so well that he knows conformity won't bring us happiness in our Christian life. That's why he tells us not to conform to the world but to be transformed.

2: Transformed? That's a fancy word for changed, isn't it?

1: Yes. God wants us to change and the only way we can change and become the living sacrifice he wants is by putting our mind on him. When we look at God instead of at the world, our desire becomes to do the will of God.

2: And the will of God is that we become living sacrifices?

1: Say, you figure things out pretty fast.

2: You know, when I think about it, it would be easier to become a dead sacrifice.

1: How do you come up with that?

2: Well, you'd only have to die one time and it would all be over. But this living sacrifice bit—it's so...so...

1: Daily?

2: You got it!

1: But it's the only sacrifice that is acceptable to God.

2: I really want to offer an acceptable sacrifice.

1: Then you'll do it?

2: Yes, I'll live for God—each day of my life. I'll become a living sacrifice—no longer conformed to the world but transformed by putting my mind on God. After all, it's the only reasonable way to serve him.

1: And the only way to prove what is the good, acceptable, and perfect will of God.

END

Talk to Me!

SCENE 1: SUPERFICIAL

CHRISSY: Hi.

LIZ: Hi.

CHRISSY: How's it going?

LIZ: Okay; how are you?

CHRISSY: Fine...ah...nice day, huh?

LIZ: Yeah...real nice.

CHRISSY: Seems like a great day for the beach.

LIZ: Really—I was just about to say the same thing.

CHRISSY: Say, did the Cubs (add your own team) win yesterday?

LIZ: Yeah...five to three in the ninth inning. Didn't you see the game?

CHRISSY: No—my TV's broken.

LIZ: Well...I guess I'll see ya later.

CHRISSY: Okay. See ya. *(walks away)*

SCENE 2: GOSSIP

CHRISSY: Hi.

LIZ: Hi. How's it going?

CHRISSY: Oh, okay. How are you?

LIZ: Fine...Say, did you hear about George?

CHRISSY: George...you mean George E.?

LIZ: Yeah, that George.

CHRISSY: No...what happened?

LIZ: Well...I don't know...and I wouldn't repeat this, because I promised not to say anything to anyone but...

CHRISSY: But what?

LIZ: Well, you gotta promise you won't tell anyone first.

CHRISSY: Okay, I promise and I cross my heart. *(crosses heart)*

LIZ: Okay. Well, Barb told me that George is not going back to school this fall.

CHRISSY: How come?

LIZ: He flunked out last semester. At least that's what I heard.

CHRISSY: Well, that's not so bad; I can think of worse things that can happen.

LIZ: No, wait—there's more. He dropped out because he got a girl pregnant.

CHRISSY: Oh, I see.

LIZ: And the reason he got her pregnant was that they were out partying and he drank too much. I mean he really got blitzed and he couldn't control himself, and one thing led to another, and bang—she's expecting.

CHRISSY: You're kidding!

LIZ: No! And I guess the girl is a real dog! She's so ugly they call her E.T.

CHRISSY: Gee...what a bummer!

LIZ: Well, hey, I gotta go...but now, remember, don't tell anybody else about this, okay?

CHRISSY: Oh, no, I won't...I promise.

LIZ: Okay. See ya later. *(exits, SHARON enters)*

CHRISSY: Hi. How's it going?

SHARON: Okay. Hey, what's up?

CHRISSY: Not much...Hey, did you hear about George?

SHARON: No...what happened?

CHRISSY: Well, you're not going to believe this...but you gotta promise you won't tell anybody...*(both exit)*

SCENE 3: OPINION

CHRISSY: I know I'm a little overweight; I should go on a diet.

LIZ: I know how you feel; I put on 10 pounds after my sister's wedding and I feel lousy.

SHARON: Well, I know all about fitness. I run every day, and I know it's the best thing for me. I know I'm really healthy.

CHRISSY: I wish there were some way I could get into better shape. Maybe I do need some exercise.

SHARON: Hey, try running—it's excellent aerobic exercise. I run every day and I feel terrific. In fact, I've read several books by running experts—you know, stuff by Cooper and Fixx. Real authorities.

LIZ: Well maybe what Chrissy needs right now is just a little self confidence to boost her ego.

SHARON: Confidence. I know all about that. I've run two marathons and about 25 road races over the past two years. It takes a lot of confidence to complete a 26.2-mile marathon, you know. And I even did it under four hours. It was a terrific feeling.

CHRISSY: Gee. I could never run 26 miles. I probably couldn't even finish one lap around the track. I'm really out of shape.

SHARON: Hey, I know about being in shape! I went to a week-long running camp once. It was great. I got up at 6:30 every morning for our morning workout. Then we had talks on running, nutrition, physiology, injuries, stretching, and workouts. It was fantastic.

LIZ: Well, Chrissy, maybe you should start out small—like an aerobics class at the YMCA. They offer all kinds of fitness programs for beginners. They even have a swimming pool.

SHARON: Swimming? Great sport! I remember last year when I was in the triathlon. We had to swim a quarter mile for the first part. Then we had a 10-mile bike ride and a four-mile run. What a challenge! But I finished in an hour and six minutes.

CHRISSY: Gee, I can't swim, either. I guess I can't do anything. Now I'm depressed—what a bummer. This is the pits—let's go get a pizza.

LIZ: I'll go with you. You seem like you need a little company and some cheering up. Are you coming, Sharon?

SHARON: Oh no. I'm on a special training diet, getting in shape for a 10-K run next week, and I want to set a new record. I'm staying away from junk food. You are what you eat, you know.

CHRISSY & LIZ: Okay. See ya.

SHARON: Bye. *(over her shoulder as she exits)* Hey, don't forget to pray for me next week during my race.

SCENE 4: FEELING

CHRISSY: Well we've been on retreat quite a while already. How do you think it's going?

LIZ: Well...to be honest, I was really scared at first.

SHARON: Why's that?

LIZ: Well...I thought everyone else would know all the others, and I felt like I was the only one who came by myself.

CHRISSY: Oh really?

LIZ: Yeah. I was almost ready to turn around and go home last night —I just felt so out of it.

SHARON: Hmmmm...I think I understand how you feel. I know my first retreat was the same way. I was a sophomore in high school. I didn't know how I got there, and I didn't know anybody. It took me a while to warm up to people.

CHRISSY: Yeah. Give yourself some more time. I think talking about how you feel helps, too. I know if I don't let people know how I'm feeling at times, they never know. I think I expect them to know—but they can't read my mind.

SHARON: That's right—me, too. I think I'm a lot more honest with myself if I can let people know how I'm feeling. Lots of times it's hard because I never know how the other person is going to react—whether she's going to be open and really listen to me.

LIZ: You mean you're afraid they might reject you and think you're weird or something?

SHARON: That's it.

CHRISSY: I know what you mean. Why do we do that to one another? I'm sure I've turned people off before, when I should have taken time to listen to them. *(pause)*

LIZ: *(to the audience)* Do you feel like we're really listening to you? And trying to be understanding? How do you really feel about the retreat so far?

END

MISSIONS MICROCOSM

At a small table on the platform, four speakers sit with microphones. They carry on a conversation similar to the one below.

JASMINE: You all have a copy of next year's budget and projections. What do you think?

DREW: This is the same as last year's! All of our costs have gone up! And we need to send out more people! How can we keep the same figures as last year?

ABBY: He's right. Transportation, printing, equipment are all way up from last year. And food costs have skyrocketed in the Philippines and Irian Jaya because of the droughts. How can we expect our missionaries to get by on this? Let alone expand their ministries!

JASMINE: You all know that we've had trouble making our budget these last few years. If the money doesn't come in, we can't spend it. It's been a step of faith even to come up with this budget, yet we're confident that God will supply. But it will mean sacrifice.

WAYNE: The people in our churches give to missions and God has blessed our work so far. But some still don't see missions as being very important.

DREW: Don't they see the need? Don't they understand the number of lost souls out there?

WAYNE: Well, probably not. We try our best to educate the churches, but remember—most of them haven't had the kind of exposure to overseas missions we have. Most don't realize how many are lost.

JASMINE: On top of that, some are hesitant to give to missions because they don't think they can afford it.

WAYNE: Or else they feel that we have enough missionaries now.

ABBY: Enough missionaries...enough missionaries. Hmm...Jesus said, "The harvest is plentiful but the workers are few." I guess that's still true today.

DREW: In Bogota we have eight missionary families in a city of almost three million. We have only two missionaries in Bombay, and 18 in the entire Upper Volta! Even with the national pastors and evangelists, it's a huge task. There are so many people...

ABBY: And so many forces are working against us—paganism, cults...

JASMINE: God has called us to a difficult task; there's no doubt about that. But he's also promised to equip us for that task. Nothing is impossible when we're in God's will.

ABBY: That's right.

DREW: I wish people would stop seeing missions as an extra—or as something for somebody else to do. Jesus told us to go. If we can't go ourselves, we can at least support those who go.

WAYNE: Well, Jesus also told us to pray that God would send laborers into his harvest. Let's pray that the Holy Spirit will work in the churches. He can convince people of the needs much better than we can. If he does, and people listen, we will be able to expand the work.

END

RENT-A-CHRISTIAN

The skit on page 103 can be used effectively to open up a good discussion about what a real Christian looks like. Feel free to adapt the script or add other "model" Christians as you see fit. Dress each character appropriately.

WHOP THAT WORK!

Here's a fun skit (page 104) that will help kids to understand better the concept of grace and faith in Christ. Set it up like a TV game show. *Esther Hetrick*

DESIGNER CROSSES

The sermon-skit about discipleship (on page 106) in the form of a fashion show takes some preparation. Although this script calls for all roles to be played by females, adjust it any way you want to accommodate

your group's personality and size. The models should dress and walk like high-fashion models, and their clothes should also suggest what they represent.

Mindy Kiser, Heidi Folkertsma, and Gary Lowe

TAKE UP YOUR CROSS

This six-scene drama (page 108) can comprise an entire evening's program. Allow enough preparation time to memorize lines, rehearse, and make the props. *James L. Wing*

HI! I'M HABAKKUK

This skit—based on the little-read prophecy of Habakkuk, a fascinating book that is actually very relevant to students today—opens discussion about faith and questioning God. See page 113. *Lisa Andersen*

SAMARITAN RAP

A New Testament story in rap is on page 115. It's especially appropriate for children's sermons performed by you or your high schoolers to the accompaniment of a rap track or to a couple of people who can vocalize the rhythm-heavy, percussive rapping sound. *Lyn Wargny*

GOLIATH RAP

And still another rap, this time from the Old Testament. Turn to page 117. *Lyn Wargny*

GUILTY!

Christ paid the penalty for our sins, this skit illustrates (page 119). *Rob Peterson*

WILLY THE PRODIGAL

The actors in your group may either read or memorize the lines to this humorous retelling of the parable of the prodigal son (page 120). Even the audience gets involved when the narrator holds up various cue cards. *Kyle Goodsey*

Rent-a-Christian

CHARACTERS
•Narrator •Salesman •Shopper •4 Christian "models"

NARRATOR: Choose means to select, to prefer, to decide...it means making those selections and decisions that have to be made—like whatcha gonna do with your life? We have lots of choices ahead of us—just like this shopper.

SALESMAN: Welcome to our Rent-A-Christian showroom. We have a wide selection to choose from, all at reasonable rates! If you'll come right this way. Let's begin with Model #6052, what we fondly call our C.E. model—Christmas and Easter. This model lasts for years, because you only use it twice a year. On these important occasions when you need to be in church, send the C.E. model in your place. It comes in all ages, styles, and colors.

SHOPPER: Hmmmm. Very nice, but I was thinking of something I could use a little more often.

SALESMAN: Of course. Then, let's look at Model #0411, our Looking Good model. Made of inexpensive materials, this model is designed especially for Sundays—it has the durability to make it through Sunday school, church, and evening worship without a hitch. It doesn't function well during the week, but our customers have been very pleased with its Sunday performance.

SHOPPER: Do you have anything a little more...uh, convenient? I mean, I'm not sure I want to be tied down every Sunday.

SALESMAN: I know just the thing! Right this way...this is #1553, a very popular model. We call it our Hit-and-Miss model. This model can

say and do the right thing on most any occasion; it grew up in the church so it has a good background, but it's not always predictable. It may or may not show up each week, but in general it gives a good impression and is well liked by all. It also comes with a special feature. It can create the perfect excuse for anything in under 30 seconds—a very popular item!

SHOPPER: Yes, that would be nice. But what is that one over there in the corner?

SALESMAN: Oh...well, that one. You probably wouldn't be interested in that one. #0012 is rather a rare breed. Some have dubbed it the "Real Thing." It's deeply involved in church life, but even more involved in living out its convictions on a daily basis. It doesn't always mix well with others, because it tends to stand out for its peculiarities, but it can always be counted on for its consistency and dedication. This one is harder to find—we have to special-order it, and it does cost more than the others.

SHOPPER: I see. You have quite a selection here.

SALESMAN: I should tell you that due to the nature of our products, we regret that we cannot offer a warranty, because we do not know when their "number will come up," so to speak. Have you chosen the model you would like?

SHOPPER: Oh, dear, I can't decide. It's such a hard choice...*(they walk off together).*

END

Whop That Work!

CHARACTERS

•Wanda Whiteheart (announcer) •Wendy Wellwisher (host) •Larry Liveright (contestant 1) •Becky Begood (contestant 2)

WANDA: Welcome to "Whop That Work," the game show in which contestants compete for the winning work that will win them a one-way ticket to paradise. And now, here's your host, Weeeeeeennndy Wellwisher!

WENDY: Thank you, ladies and gentlemen! Have we got a show for you today! Let me introduce our two contestants for today. Let's give a warm welcome to...Larry Liveright and Becky Begood. *(applause)* Before we get started, here's Wanda Whiteheart to tell us about our first prize.

WANDA: Thank you, Wendy. The winner of "Whop That Work" this week will win a wonderful trip. First, our winner will fly the friendly skies of the Angelic Northern Airline till he or she reaches the Pearly Gates, then he or she will walk the golden streets and stay at the Hilton on the Hilltop, a mansion built for you! That's right, our winner will receive a one-way trip to heaven! (This trip provided by Heavenly Hosts, Inc. Have you visited the best-built in Heaven lately?) Back to you, Wendy.

WENDY: Thanks, Wendy. Larry, let's start with you. What fantastic work have you done that you can share with us?

(At this point, the contestants go back and forth, trying to top the other's great deed; Wendy can interject an occasional "That's great..." and "Inspiring!" and the audience should be encouraged to get involved by clapping for their choice. The contestants can come up with their own list of works ahead of time; the more ridiculous the better. Here are a few suggestions:

• *"I picked up two hitchhikers on my way to work...and they were none too clean! It made me five minutes late for work."*

• *"I bought a Christian bumper sticker for my car. It says, HONK EIGHT TIMES IF YOU KNOW JESUS. It's a real witness wherever I go."*

• *"I went with the youth group to McDonald's—we all wore our matching Christian T-shirts. Talk about large-scale evangelism."*

• *"I memorized the steps of salvation. The next time someone comes up to me and asks me, 'What must I do to be saved?' I'll be ready."*

As the show progresses, the contestants should get increasingly rude to each other, until Wendy calls a halt)

WENDY: Hate to stop—we're just getting warmed up, but we're almost out of time. We'll give the judges a moment to choose the winner, and while they're doing that, I'd like to take this opportunity to thank our contestants for being on the show, and wish them both the best. Ah, the judges have reached a verdict. *(reaches for an envelope)* And the winner is...Folks, this has never happened before— we have a tie! Let me read the scores—Larry Liveright...zero; Becky Begood...zero! *(everyone freezes)*

VOICE: "For it is by grace you have been saved, through faith—and this is not from yourselves; it is the gift of God—and not by works, so that no one can boast" (Ephesians 2:8-9).

END

105

✝✝✝✝✝✝✝✝✝✝✝✝✝✝✝✝✝✝✝✝✝✝✝✝✝✝✝✝

DESIGNER CROSSES

CHARACTERS

- 2 Commentators

- 5 Models

- 5 Crosses, made of heavy cardboard or plywood:

- "Comfy Cross," padded and covered with blue-and-white gingham

- "Holiday Cross," a silk poinsettia and Easter lily are taped to it

- "Upwardly Mobile Cross," painted gray and covered with plastic and glass "jewels," with credit cards and BMW stickers, etc., pasted on it

- "Crisis Cross," a small pocket cross

- "Original Cross," a large, rough, wooden cross; its model has a blue-collar look about him or her, obviously a person who serves rather than supervises…maybe wears overalls

---

1ST COMMENTATOR: Ladies and gentlemen, admirers of high fashion—we want to welcome you to the first showing of this year's line of designer crosses. We understand that some of you are new to our line of specialty crosses, so permit us to describe our product. We want you to share our enthusiasm for how we clothe the Christian community in America.

2ND COMMENTATOR: Designer crosses are specially designed crosses for the Christian who wants to make a faith statement—without, of course, offending anyone or giving neighbors reason to think we're too fanatical or radical. We're an old company—we opened our first outlet back in the first century in that wild, crazy, fun town of Corinth. Our business has flourished ever since—except for those occasional recessions when Christians are called back to spiritual renewal based on living out their faith in word and deed. Sales do suffer at such times, but only temporarily. We have always quickly rebounded from such setbacks, and we are currently doing a booming business, especially with the present generation.

But enough of our history. Let's get to this year's fashionable line of designer crosses.

1ST COMMENTATOR: Our first cross tonight was a top seller during the eighties, and is still our most popular—our Upwardly Mobile Cross. Modeling our cross today is Gloria Van Shallow of Las Vegas. The Upwardly Mobile Cross appeals to the trendy Christian in all of us. If the church is the best place to be seen in town, then this cross is for you. It's tastefully decorated with symbols of power and control—a cross that lets your worldly friends know that you're really okay after all. With this cross you'll never have to think about your faith or be bothered by the needs of others around you. Thank you, Gloria.

2ND COMMENTATOR: Our second cross is the ever-popular Comfy Cross. Modeling the Comfy Cross is Wendy Y. Risk. Wendy shows us a cross for the Christian who is looking for a comfortable faith. If you're longing for no challenges, no disappointments, the Comfy Cross is for you. Pretty and fluffy, this cross comforts and

✝✝✝✝✝✝✝✝✝✝✝✝✝✝✝✝✝✝✝✝✝✝✝✝✝✝✝✝

protects its owner from all the troubles of the world—especially those tensions that are part of being a Christian in a fallen world. Want to live out your faith in a continually pleasant and protective bubble? Order this cross today. Thanks, Wendy.

1ST COMMENTATOR: Here is Ms. Scarcely B. Seen modeling our traditional Holiday Cross. Although the market segment that traditionally purchases this designer cross is not here tonight, we thought we'd give you a sneak preview anyway. Notice the seasonal touch, thanks to the silk Easter lily and satin poinsettia.

2ND COMMENTATOR: Now we introduce the new pocket-size Crisis Cross, modeled by Tina C. Trouble. The Crisis Cross is exceptionally popular among students at exam time, among motorists in fender benders, soldiers in foxholes, white water canoeists who lose their paddles in class-five rapids, and lost children in malls. The popularity of this cross is due to its minute size—it can be hidden until a crisis arrives, until you need divine intervention. Until then—while your life is running smoothly—the pocket Crisis Cross can rest safely in your pocket. No one will even suspect you have one. Thanks, Tina.

1ST COMMENTATOR: Our final designer cross tonight doesn't sell well, doesn't look hot—but we thought we'd pull it out to give you a look at the prototype for all our designer crosses, the Original Cross. Of course, as you've seen tonight, we've improved on it immensely through the years. We don't get a lot of calls for it anymore. As a matter of fact, our advertising firm is pushing us to drop this cross. After exhaustive market research, they have concluded that this cross simply doesn't suit an individualistic culture.

Not to mention the demands this cross makes on its owners. This cross requires that its owners deny themselves, sacrifice themselves, serve others and their needs, love their enemies, speak and live nothing but the truth, walk the extra mile for others, be fiercely loyal and faithful at all costs to the One who first carried this cross.

2ND COMMENTATOR: Yet some fashion critics have pointed out that, though it's not as flashy as our designer crosses, it does have simple lines and carries a clear statement. And we cannot deny that, however poorly it sells, its customer-satisfaction rating is phenomenal. The few who own one tell us of a deep contentment that this cross and its demands brought to their lives. In the opinion of some, the warranty more than compensates for its plain looks. Although most of our best-selling crosses come with one-year guarantees—and a few with lifetime guarantees—the original cross comes with an eternal guarantee.

So which cross will you take up today? We hope you consider purchasing from the prestigious line of designer crosses.

END

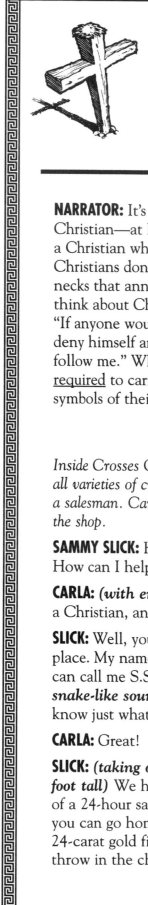

Take Up Your Cross

CHARACTERS
•Narrator •Carla •Sammy Slick •Simon •Matt •Tom
•Megan •Jenny •3 or 4 teenagers

NARRATOR: It's fairly easy to be a Christian—at least, it's easy to <u>say</u> you're a Christian when it's convenient. Christians don't have signs around their necks that announce their faith. But think about Christ's words in Mark 8:34: "If anyone would come after me, he must deny himself and take up his cross and follow me." What if Christians were <u>required</u> to carry crosses as mandatory symbols of their faith?

SCENE 1

Inside Crosses Galore, a mall shop that sells all varieties of crosses. Behind the counter is a salesman. Carla, a new Christian, enters the shop.

SAMMY SLICK: Hel-lo. Come in, come in. How can I help you?

CARLA: *(with enthusiasm)* I just became a Christian, and I'd like to get a cross.

SLICK: Well, you've come to the right place. My name is Sammy Slick, but you can call me S.S. *(making a hissing, snake-like sound)* I'm your friend—and I know just what you need.

CARLA: Great!

SLICK: *(taking out a gold cross about a foot tall)* We happen to be in the middle of a 24-hour sale, and for only $24.95 you can go home wearing this beautiful 24-carat gold filigree cross. We'll even throw in the chain.

CARLA: *(hesitating)* Oh...well, this isn't quite what I was looking for...

SLICK: I understand. It's too big. I know exactly how you feel. *(pulls out a tiny cross)* Listen, here's a little sweetheart that I can let go for $19.95. The chain is extra, but I'll give you a good deal.

CARLA: *(shaking her head, trying to be polite)* No...I don't think—

SLICK: Okay. The chain's included—but that deal's good only today.

CARLA: No. You see, I'm looking for something bigger than that.

SLICK: Gotcha! *(from behind the counter, he pulls out a huge, four- or five-foot garish, gaudy, glittery cross)* This is a very popular style, though of course it does run a bit more.

CARLA: Maybe you don't understand. I guess it's not the <u>size</u> of the cross as much as... Well, when my friends became Christians, they carried big crosses, but they were rough, unpainted, plain wooden crosses. I thought they were crazy, but now I think I understand. Do you have anything in stock like that? Maybe this big? *(gestures size)*

SLICK: You know, I used to carry those, but they moved so slow that I discontinued that model. Hardly anyone wants to buy those. Most people just rent 'em—for those special occasions when you need to look the part, you see—and then return them.

CARLA: Can you tell me a store that does sell them?

SLICK: *(pauses, considers Carla carefully while stroking his chin)* Well, I really shouldn't do this, but you look determined. I'll draw you a map. Here's where you can find them. *(he quickly sketches out a map on a scrap of paper)* It's called The Cross Shop, corner of Fifth and Main. The guy doesn't do much business, but he may have what you're looking for.

CARLA: Thanks! *(exits, passing two others entering the shop)*

SLICK: Hel-lo. Come in, come in. How can I help you today? *(lights out)*

SCENE 2

The Cross Shop. A counter behind which is a row of only one kind of cross—big wooden ones. A salesman is behind the counter.

SIMON: Hello. My name is Simon. Can I help you?

CARLA: My name is Carla and I just became a Christian. I'd like to buy a cross. *(looks at the display of crosses)* These are perfect...just what I've been looking for.

SIMON: Sure this is what you want?

CARLA: Positive. When I met Jesus, I was told that the cross of Christ would bring me tests and hardship as well as great joy. But I know that God will give me the strength I need and that he'll never leave me.

SIMON: Sounds like you're a determined young lady. This the one you want? *(Carla nods, and Simon hands her the cross)* There you go.

CARLA: How much do I owe you?

SIMON: Nothing.

CARLA: Nothing?

SIMON: Not right now, at least.

CARLA: But I was just at Crosses Galore, and Mr. Slick told me that—

SIMON: I know. Some people think they can buy their salvation like that. They're wrong. You begin paying when you carry it out the door.

CARLA: Thanks, Simon. By the way, how'd you ever get into this line of work?

SIMON: My family's been in this business a long time. An ancestor of mine—after whom I'm named—opened the first shop in Cyrene. His first cross was a lot like the one you have there. *(if biblical literacy is not your group's strong suit, at this point Simon may read Matthew 27:32: "As they were going out, they met a man from Cyrene, named Simon, and they forced him to carry the cross")* Now that you have your cross, I'd like to pass along something a missionary once said. His name was Jim Elliot. "He is no fool who gives what he cannot keep to gain what he cannot lose." Maybe that'll help you.

CARLA: *(thoughtfully)* Thanks, Simon. *(exits, lights out)*

SCENE 3

School hallway, lockers in the background. Students are between classes. A group of three or four teenagers enter stage right, carrying books, chatting, laughing, etc., walk across stage and exit stage left—just as Megan and Jenny enter stage left.

MEGAN: *(enthusiastically)* Isn't this exciting? Tomorrow is the last day of school!

JENNY: I can't wait. I'm gonna par-ty this summer. Hey, I like your top.

MEGAN: Thanks. I got it at the mall last night. Hey, did Dave call you last night? Karen told me he was going to— *(Matt and Tom enter and interrupt)*

TOM: Hey, don't talk about the big party tonight without including us! What's happenin'?

MEGAN: Not much. Speaking of party animals *(she gives Tom a playful shove)*, did you hear that Carla became a Christian? I can't believe that someone who lived the way she did could be good enough to go to <u>our</u> church.

MATT: I heard that she's way too serious about it. One of my friends saw her at The Cross Shop. You wouldn't believe what she did. First Car—

TOM: *(interrupting)* Shhh! Here she comes. *(the group of teenagers all pretend to be doing something else)*

CARLA: *(enters with her big cross)* Hi, everyone. I guess you heard I became a Christian.

MEGAN: Yes, that's great! *(Megan's actual thought, spoken by an offstage voice, perhaps with a microphone)* I can't believe she's carrying that ugly cross.

TOM: We're really happy for you. *(Tom's actual thought, spoken by an offstage voice)* I've got to get out of here before everyone sees me with her and starts laughing.

MATT: You'll have to come to the next youth meeting at our church. *(spoken by an offstage voice)* I hope she decides to go to a different church.

JENNY: I heard the bad news about Brad. It must have been hard breaking up with him because he's not a Christian. *(spoken by an offstage voice)* Maybe he'll ask <u>me</u> out now.

CARLA: Yeah, it was hard. But it was the best way to go. I hope he'll become a Christian, too. Maybe you guys can witness to him.

ALL: Sure, sure. *(spoken by an offstage voice)* No way we could do that. We'd feel so stupid.

CARLA: Speaking of witnessing, where's your crosses? *(everyone reveals a tiny cross, worn in an inconspicuous place—except Matt, who keeps looking for his during the next few moments, and finally gives up looking)* They are nice...but isn't it hard for people to see them?

MEGAN: Well...maybe...but if people look hard enough they can see them fine.

TOM: Besides, we don't want people to get the wrong first impression.

MATT: When we first became Christians, we all had crosses like yours, Carla. But it was so hard to witness to our friends because those humongous crosses really irritated them. They finally avoided us—or laughed at us.

JENNY: Or both.

TOM: This way, if we don't want people to know that we're—I mean, we can share our faith when we want to...you know, when the time is right. *(Everyone but Carla nods in agreement. The bell rings and they all rush off, leaving Carla standing alone and looking puzzled. Lights out)*

SCENE 4

A big sign in the background says PARTY, with an arrow pointing offstage, stage right. A smaller sign reads PARK YOUR CROSS, 50¢. Matt, Tom, Megan, and Jenny enter from stage left and go to center stage.

TOM: *(to Matt)* Hey, your cross is showing.

MATT: Oh, thanks. I forgot all about it. *(puts his necklace inside his shirt)*

CARLA: *(approaching with her big cross)* Hi, guys!

MEGAN: Look, Carla, why don't you leave your cross outside before we go in to the party. It would look...uh, better that way.

CARLA: What do you mean?

MEGAN: Well, there might be some...uh, drinking, maybe, and stuff going on...

CARLA: You mean you guys are going to—

JENNY: We're just going to the party to have a good time. All our friends are there. That thing *(pointing to the cross)* might bother some people. It will probably just get in the way of things. *(Another teenager—with a cross just like Carla's—enters stage left, parks his cross under the* PARK YOUR CROSS *sign, then heads out stage right toward the party)*

TOM: It's not that hard to do, Carla. Think about it. *(all but Carla exit toward the party)*

CARLA: *(to herself, but aloud)* But shouldn't it be hard to do? *(lights out)*

SCENE 5

Next day, Mexican restaurant. Matt, Tom, Megan, and Jenny are sitting around a table waiting for the waitress to bring their lunch. Tom is playing with packages of hot sauce. Megan has a squirt gun.

MEGAN: Wasn't that a great party last night?

JENNY: It was super! *(to Matt)* Hey, what's wrong?

MEGAN: I think he's had too much hot sauce. This will cool him off! *(takes out her squirt gun and shoots him. Everyone laughs—except Matt)*

JENNY: What's wrong? Still worried you won't graduate? I heard Mr. Keller's final was really tough.

MATT: No, it's not that. I just...well, I'm thinking about going back to my old cross.

TOM: What? That big hunk of hardwood? C'mon, you've been studying too hard. I think your brain's burned out.

MATT: No, I'm serious. I've been thinking about it a lot lately.

MEGAN: You can't do this to us. We've got a great summer ahead of us—the four of us.

TOM: We haven't got room for that cross—and besides...oh, I get it. You'll only carry it to church and maybe to youth group, right?

MATT: No, I want it with me all the time. I know it'll get in the way, but I've gotta do it. I've been watching Carla the last couple of days. She reminds me of how things used to be with me. When I first became a Christian, I was proud to carry that cross around. I couldn't read my Bible enough, I couldn't wait to tell my friends about Jesus.

JENNY: But we've got our crosses. They're just more convenient than the big model, and they accomplish the same thing.

MATT: Do they? When was the last time someone noticed your cross, Jenny? When was the last time any of us explained to someone what the cross meant?

MEGAN: But Jesus never said the cross had to be big.

MATT: Yeah, but the cross Jesus carried and was crucified on wasn't gold-plated. You couldn't wear it around your neck. It was heavy and splintery. It caused him pain. It was work for him to carry it. I think it should be the same for us.

TOM: I think your brain is bummed out. *(the girls laugh and nod in agreement. Lights out)*

SCENE 6

School hallway, the next day. Matt, Tom, Megan, and Jenny enter stage right, talking. When Matt notices Carla entering stage left—carrying her big cross—he leaves the other three to talk with her. The three continue walking and exit stage left.

MATT: Carla! Am I glad to see you. I've got something to tell you.

CARLA: What is it?

MATT: *(takes a big breath)* I've decided to take up the cross I used to have when I first became a Christian.

CARLA: I don't understand.

MATT: You reminded me of the way I used to be when I first met Christ. Not ashamed of my faith, wherever I went, no matter who I was with. I want that again—thanks to you, Carla.

CARLA: I...I don't know what to say. I mean...I've been doing a lot of thinking. That's why I was late to first period today. I was wondering if it was even worth carrying this cross anymore. But I decided to stay with it.

MATT: Why?

CARLA: I remembered something that Simon—well, this guy I got my cross from, he told me something a missionary once said: "He is no fool who gives what he cannot keep to gain what he cannot lose."

MATT: I'm glad you didn't give up, Carla. *(bell rings)*

CARLA: See you Sunday at youth group?

MATT: Wouldn't miss it! *(begins walking away, but stops at Carla's next word)*

CARLA: Hey. *(pause)* I love you, brother.

MATT: Love you, too. *(the two hug, then exit. Lights out)*

(A voice offstage with a microphone reads Mark 8:34-38:

> *Calling to the crowd to join his disciples, he said, "Anyone who intends to come with me has to let me lead. You're not in the driver's seat; I am. Don't run from suffering; embrace it. Follow me and I'll show you how. Self-help is no help at all. Self-sacrifice is the way, my way, to saving yourself, your true self. What good would it do to get everything you want and lose you, the real you? What could you ever trade your soul for?*

> *If any of you are embarrassed over me and the way I'm leading you when you get around your fickle and unfocused friends, know that you'll be an even greater embarrassment to the Son of Man when he arrives in all the splendor of God, his Father, with an army of the holy angels.")*

Scripture passage from *The Message: The New Testament in Contemporary Language*, translated by Eugene H. Peterson (NavPress, 1993)

END

Hi! I'm Habakkuk

CHARACTERS
•Narrator •Habakkuk •God

NARRATOR: Tonight we tell you the story of the prophet Habakkuk—one of the minor prophets we don't hear much about. In fact, unless you're a real whiz at memorizing the books of the Bible, you may not even know where to find Habakkuk's book. I'll give you a clue: it's between Nahum and Zephaniah. Does that help? Habakkuk had a curious encounter with God that we can learn from. Here to tell you more about it is the man himself—Habakkuk.

HABAKKUK: Hi, I'm Habakkuk. Some of my friends call me Hab. Before I tell you about what I wrote in my book, I should tell you a bit about myself. Frankly, there isn't a whole lot that anyone knows about me. Some think I was a Levite and a temple musician; others say I was from the tribe of Simeon. At any rate, I lived and wrote shortly before the Babylonian invasion of Judah, which would be about 610 b.c.

NARRATOR: Before we get started with our story, a little background will help. At the time Hab wrote, Judah was not a happy place. The nation was wicked, the sin of its people was blatant, its leaders corrupt, they weren't seeking God—and they weren't even ashamed. The Babylonians were a constant threat, violence and injustice reigned, evil always overwhelmed good, and God seemed very distant and without much control of the situation.

HABAKKUK: I was really upset by all that I saw going on around me. After all, this was God's nation, his people. The bad were getting away with murder, and the good were being sucked in. Being an up-front guy, I went to God and—well, it's a little embarrassing to admit—but I complained. "God," I demanded, "how long do I have to watch this evil? How long must I ask you for help and get no response? Where is your punishment for all this wrongdoing?"

GOD: No, I wasn't upset that Hab had come to me with his worries and complaints, because he really wanted to understand my truth about the situation. But I wanted him to know that I was in charge—though not in the way he expected. My answer to his questions, though, confused him. "I am going to deal with the evil and violence in the land," I told him, "but not in the way you think. I'm letting those cruel Babylonians conquer Judah."

HABAKKUK: This was more than I could take. The Babylonians?! Of all people! What did God think he was doing? Sure, there were problems among God's people—sure, they had abandoned God and pursued their own ways—sure, they were wrong and deserved punishment. But from the Babylonians?! I mean, they were so much worse than even we were. "Are you out of your mind?" I asked God. "You're too pure and holy to even look at evil like the Babylonians. How can you use them to punish us when they are much worse than us? Something's not right here, and I'm going up to the tower to wait for your answer."

GOD: I told Hab that judgment would come—judgment on Judah through the Babylonians, then judgment on the Babylonians by me. Evil would be repaid in specific ways, but in my timing and according to my plan. He would have to wait to see the final results and trust me to take care of judgment.

HABAKKUK: When I heard these last words of God, I finally became quiet and did the first smart thing I had done that day—I prayed. I remembered all the times God had shown himself to us. I reminded myself of how God had cared for his people through history and had brought justice in times of wickedness. I was scared of the promised invasion, but I was convinced that God was in charge and that he would take care of revenge and injustice. The more I thought about God's goodness and faithfulness in the past, the more I knew that I would trust him, regardless of what the present looked like. He alone was my God and he alone would be my strength.

NARRATOR: And that's Hab's story. I should probably add this: the Babylonians attacked Jerusalem—just as God said they would—in 605 b.c., and Jerusalem shortly fell and the Israelites were exiled to Babylon. Within 70 years, however—and according to God's word to Habakkuk—the Babylonians were themselves conquered by Persia.

END

Samaritan Rap

This Jewish dude was going down the road to Jericho.

A robber, who was hiding, jumped right out and shouted, "Yo!

Don't even think of running, pal, and don't try nothin' funny.

Don't give me any trouble, pal, just give me all your money."

The Jewish dude was frightened. "Oh, have mercy, please!" he said,

But the robber beat him badly, and then left the dude for dead.

Now, a couple hours later, this priest guy came along.

His mind was on the temple and he hummed a holy song.

He thought he loved the Lord, but when he saw the fellow lying,

He said, "Oh, dear, how awful—the dude there may be dying.

I can't touch a dead body. Besides, I don't think I know him.

So I don't need to help him." And the priest kept on a-going.

The next was a Levite, who was also quite religious.

His position in the temple was really quite prestigious.

He went to take a closer look at where the fellow lay.

"I don't want to get involved," he said, "I'll just go on my way.

I have too much to do today to stop and help some stranger.

And if the robber's still around, I'd put myself in danger.

I won't be helping anyone if I get beaten, too,

And as I said before, I've got a lot of things to do."

A little while later came along another man.

Now this dude wasn't Jewish—he was Samaritan.

The Jews thought all Samaritans were scum, or slime, or dirt.

Samaritans would be quite pleased to see a few Jews hurt.

For years Jews and Samaritans had hated one another,

But Good Sam helped the Jew as if he were a brother.

He took him to an inn and he said, "I cannot stay,

But whatever you must spend on him, I gladly will repay.

Wash him well and feed him, and then put this dude to bed.

I'll come back and pay you later. Thanks a lot," our Good Sam said.

Now Jesus told this story to teach us to be kind.

And when you have a chance to help, please bring it to your mind.

See, God loves everybody, not just those you find appealing,

And this is the message that our story is revealing.

When you see someone in trouble, you should do the best you can

To show God's love and caring, like the good Samaritan!

And now that we are finished with our rapping and our beat,

Why, every single one of you can go back to your seat.

END

Permission to photocopy this page granted for use in your own youth group. **116**

Goliath Rap

Once upon a time, when the Hebrews were at war,
Their soldiers met a foe they had never met before.
He fought for the Philistines and his name was Goliath,
And they could not defeat him, no matter how they trieth.
Goliath was a giant. He was huge and he was scary.
His face was really mean and his arms were big and hairy.

King Saul promised a reward to anyone who'd beat him,
But all of the soldiers were too petrified to meet him.
They'd start out to fight, but then quickly run away
As soon as they heard what Goliath had to say.
He said, "I'll fight you, one to one, if anyone is willing,
And victory will be determined by who does the killing.
If I win—and I know I will—then you'll be slaves of ours.
If I should lose—preposterous!—then we'll be in your powers.
I'm ready to get going; come on, let the fight begin!
Or are you all too chicken?" said Goliath with a grin.

Now David had three brothers in the army of King Saul.
His father asked if he would go and check up on them all.
He heard Goliath's threats and he saw the Hebrews fleeing,
And he could not believe that these were soldiers he was seeing.
For David, though a shepherd boy, was full of faith and courage,
He was shocked and dismayed at the soldiers' show of worriage.
"This fellow has a lot of nerve—why, he insults our God!
And none of you will stop him? I find that very odd.
Heck, I'll go out and fight him. If you agree, then I'll
Go out and beat Goliath, for God is on our side."

D-A-VID, D-A-VID, D-A-VID, yay, David!

Saul was just delighted. "Good for you, son—I approve!"
And he loaded Dave with armor till the poor kid couldn't move.
David said, "Hey, I don't need this. I don't want anything.
I'll just take five little stones and my old shepherd's sling.

D-A-VID, D-A-VID, D-A-VID, yay, David!
(Referee) Now in this corner, weighing in around 100 pounds,
David, the brave shepherd boy, going for 10 rounds.
And in the other corner, very heavy, very tall,
The Philistine called Goliath. Which one of them will fall?

(sadly) D-A-VID, D-A-VID, D-A-VID, good luck, David.

Goliath said, "You're just a kid! I hardly need my sword!"
And David said, "That might be true were it not for the Lord.
I'm doing this one for our God, his might and power to show.
Hope you have life insurance, for we will win, I know." *(Referee rings a bell)*
So David threw a little stone, and hit him in the head.
And down fell Goliath, absolutely stone-cold dead!

D-A-VID, D-A-VID, D-A-VID, YAY DAVID!!!

(Referee counts 10 and holds up David's hand) And that's how little
David slew Goliath, saved the day,
And showed his people, "Trust in God, and you will be okay."
He did it for the Lord, and not to gain fame and glory.
And so we come at last to the moral of our story.
Although you may feel helpless, and although you may be small,
With God you can do anything—anything at all.

Well, now our story's over; that's all, my friend,
So you can go sit down again.

END

Guilty!

CHARACTERS

• Bailiff (dressed in uniform if possible) • Defendant 1, Noriega Castro Sleaze
• Defendant 2, Cindy Almost Pure • Judge (in robe, holding gavel)

Scene: Courtroom of heaven

BAILIFF: All rise! The court of heaven is now in session. The honorable Creator of all that is, was, and shall be, presiding.

JUDGE: Please be seated. Defendant one, please state your name.

DEFENDANT 1: My name is Noriega Castro Sleaze, your honor. I'm guilty—I know that now. But I don't know why I'm here. I asked for your mercy and forgiveness. What gives?

JUDGE: Mr. Sleaze, everyone that's ever been born must appear before me. Bailiff, what is the sin of Mr. Sleaze?

BAILIFF: Your honor, rape, murder, drug trafficking, and jaywalking—to name only a few of his many, many sins against humanity.

JUDGE: You have been found guilty of sin, Mr. Sleaze. The penalty is death. Defendant two, please state your name.

DEFENDANT 2: My name is Cindy Almost Pure, your most wonderful honor, your holiness, sir. And I just want you to know that I'm guilty, too—I know that, and I'm sorry for what I've done. But I'm not nearly as bad as Sleaze here. My sin is nothing compared to what he has done. Besides, I go to church every Sunday, say my prayers every day, and I obey the 10 Commandments—well, most of them.

JUDGE: Bailiff, what is the sin of Miss Almost Pure?

BAILIFF: She is guilty of envy, your honor. She wanted the Mercedes 300 SL that belonged to her neighbor.

JUDGE: You have been found guilty of sin, Miss Almost Pure, and the penalty is death.

BAILIFF: *(licking his chops)* They deserve it! Now they're gonna fry!

JUDGE: Bailiff, set them free.

BAILIFF: What do you mean? I thought you said they were guilty and the sentence was death!

JUDGE: They are guilty, and the penalty is death. But the sentence has already been served. **(holds up both hands, which are marked with red nail prints)**

OFFSTAGE VOICE: For God so loved the world that he gave his one and only Son, that whoever believes in him will not die but have eternal life.

END

WILLY THE PRODIGAL

CHARACTERS
•Narrator •Willy •Sissy •Dad

PROPS

Cue-card indicators for audience participation—prep the audience to respond to specific cue cards when the cards are held up during the skit:

 "Beanhead!"

 "Wow, that's beautiful!"

 "Uh-oh"

 "Gosh, Beav—I think you really screwed up this time!"

 "Wow!"

 "Ooooohhh, ick!"

NARRATOR: For our Sunday school lesson today, we'd like you to meet a family: Dad and his two kids—Sissy and Willy.

WILLY: I don't care what you say—life is out there for the taking, and I want to take it. Now. I don't want to waste my money and my time in college.

SISSY: But what about your future?

WILLY: There is no future. **WOW** There's only today. I'm tired of wasting all my todays for a tomorrow I may never see.

SISSY: If you don't slow down and look where you're going, you'll wind up lost.

WILLY: My money will be my guide. I'll go where it takes me.

DAD: Hey, kids! What are you two arguing about?

SISSY: Oh, not much. Just life, liberty, and the pursuit of nothing.

DAD: What do you mean?

WILLY: What she means is I want my freedom, Dad. I want my half of the money you put in the bank for us.

DAD: But you haven't decided where you're going to college.

WILLY: I don't want to go to college. I want to start enjoying life before I get old and gray like you.

DAD: Pardon me?

WILLY: I mean, uh, before I get too mature to remember what living is really like. I want to live while I still look good. I want to laugh. I want to jam. I want to—

DAD: I get the point. All right, I'll give you a check for your half, but that's all you get. All the rest of the money belongs to your sister. *(pause)* You know, son, you're really hurting me. I hate to see you do this to yourself. But, as you say, it is your life and you must live it. My only hope is that you live it wisely.

WILLY: Thanks, Pop.

NARRATOR: Well, as you can probably predict, Willy went out and lived, but not wisely. He spent money right and left. First he bought a fancy sports car from a guy named Happy Sam. This tells you how wise he was being. Next he bought a new wardrobe. He didn't really look at the clothes much. He just made sure that they had a designer label and were expensive—because, he said, "to be good, you gotta look good." No swinging bachelor is complete without a swinging bachelor's pad. So Willy purchased a condominium from—guess who?—Happy Sam. Finally, Willy began "living." Caviar and lobster for breakfast, lunch, and dinner. $20 tips. **WOW** He'd go to Baskin-Robbins and buy all 31 flavors for dessert. **WOW**

Happy Sam took Willy to all the night spots, where he spent his money gambling, drinking, and dancing until dawn. Willy was so busy spending his money on "living" that he didn't notice he was running out. He went to an ATM, punched in his PIN—and got not cash but an "Insufficient Funds" notice.

The next day he opened an envelope from his bank to discover that his checks to Happy Sam had bounced. Life became even more difficult for Willy when he heard that Happy Sam had an unhappy friend named The Mongol.

Willy stopped "living" and started surviving. Happy Sam repossessed the sports car and the condo. He pawned his wardrobe for food. Things got so bad, he placed his last 10 bucks on a 20-to-one shot in a goldfish-swallowing contest. His man lost it—I mean, really lost it!

Willy was plummeting, riding an express elevator straight to the bottom of his soul. Why, thank you! He realized he had to do something fast. All the good positions in the classifieds ended with the words, "College degree a must." Willy abandoned his search for the perfect job that provided instant wealth. He accepted the first offer he got.

WILLY: SuuuuEEE! SuuuuEEE! C'mere, pig pig pig! Boy, I tell ya, those hogs are slobs—and they don't smell so sweet, either. This is horrible. I can't believe I'm working for a pig farmer, and for what he's paying me, too...those pigs eat better than I do. Of course, he did tell me I could have their leftovers. And I've been hungry enough to appreciate the offer. The only problem is that pigs don't leave leftovers. I am so depressed.

NARRATOR: Willy began crying as he walked toward the sty gate, not looking where he was going. He felt something cold and mushy on his ankles, on his knees, on his waist, his chest, his chin...he was sinking and sinking fast.

WILLY: Great...just great. This is really the pits. Here I am up to my neck in muck, and nowhere to take a bath. I am so sick of living this way. Why didn't I listen to my dad? Why didn't my sister argue with me harder? Why didn't they just tie me up and force feed me and make me go to college? I know why: because they love me. I feel so foolish. I've wasted all the money my dad worked hard to earn. I want to go back home. I want to go back in the worst way and that's just the way I'm going.

NARRATOR: Willy pulled himself out of the mud and headed home. And I've got to tell you, folks, he looked and smelled disgusting. As he walked the long walk home, people stared, children pointed fingers, and a Chihuahua bit him. He was miserable.

WILLY: I sure hope Dad and Sissy take me back, or at least let me stay in the garage. Maybe Dad could hire me as a gardener or something. Maybe if I'm lucky, Sissy will give me a dollar or two to wash her car. I am so sorry I did this. If they only knew what I went through. *(singing mournfully)* "Nobody knows the trouble I've seen..." All of this just goes to prove them right. I wish they would have just shown me pictures or a video or something that would have given me an idea of what to expect. Oh well, as my grandpappy used to tell me—"Wish in one hand, spit in the other, and see which one fills up first."

Well, here I am, Dad...Dad? It's me, your dumbest child, remember? I'm not worthy to be your son. Dad, I'm sorry. I've been a real pain in the—I mean, I've been a real jerk, Dad.

DAD: Willy...Willy, is that you?

WILLY: I'm afraid so.

DAD: Willy my son—whoa...pee-yew, you smell—and look—disgusting.

WILLY: I know, Dad. People stared at me, kids pointed at me, and a Chihuahua bit me.

DAD: Well, I'm just glad you're home. Sissy, come here! Willy's home!

SISSY: Hi, Willy! Boy, you smell—and look—disgusting.

DAD: He knows, dear. People stared at him, kids pointed at him, and a Chihuahua bit him. But he's come home! Come on, Sissy, let's take Willy out and buy him some new clothes, a new car, some dinner. How about some lobster, son?

WILLY: I think I've had enough lobster to last me a while. And if it's all right with you, no pork, either.

NARRATOR: So they took Willy out and bought him new clothes and a new car. By the way, they ate Italian that evening. Everyone was happy to see Willy back at home, but Sissy was a little upset.

SISSY: Dad, I'm really glad Willy's back and all, but I'm a little upset. He took all his money, ran off, had a good time, spent himself down to nothing, crawls back here—and look at the treatment he's getting! I've been here the whole time, I'm going to college—but you've never given me a party like this.

DAD: Look at it this way, honey. Willy didn't actually have that great of a time out there, and he's really sorry now. Besides, he's spent all his money, and you've still got most of yours. You've got a lot more than he does. What I'm trying to tell you is when someone is truly repentant and sorry for what he did, don't close the door on him. Rejoice!

NARRATOR: And that's the story of Willy the Prodigal.

END

THE PROBLEM WITH FRIENDS

Coach one of your theatrical students to give the monologue on page 124 as an introduction for a meeting on the topic of friendship—or give it yourself in teenage "costume." *Kyle White*

GOSPEL LITE

This short skit drives the point home about how much we actually desire to live out a radical gospel.
Brad Fulton

BUD: After a hard night of partyin'... *(crushes an empty beer can and tosses it away)*

BUTCH: ...carousin'... *(does the same)*

BUD: ...and chasin' ladies... *(belches)*

BUTCH: ...me and Bud like to get right with a nice dose of Gospel Lite. *(holds up a special Bible the size of a small paperback from which pages have obviously been removed)* It has all the love, blessings, and prosperity you've come to expect in the gospel—with only half the commitment. It feels great!

BUD: *(grabs Bible from Butch and holds it up)* What Butch means is that Gospel Lite doesn't cramp our lifestyle. We can still enjoy all our old friends, hit all the parties, and live it up like we always did. And it won't slow us down because it's a lot less filling than the real gospel.

BUTCH: *(grabs Bible back)* That's true, Bud. But what the people will really like is that they can not only enjoy all the sins of their former life, but all the fruits of God's blessing, too. Gospel Lite feels great!

BUD: *(snatches back the Bible)* That may be so, Butch, but what you'll like best is that Gospel Lite has less commitment than the regular gospel. You can still keep up with the rest of the world without getting weighted down by a lot of heavy responsibilities. If you don't like something it says, just tear it out! Gospel Lite is less filling!

BUTCH: *(yanks Bible fiercely from Bud)* No, Bud, Gospel Lite is full of blessings—heaven, healing, and financial prosperity! It feels great!

BUD: *(this time Bud is too slow, and Butch keeps it barely out of arm's reach as Bud makes desperate attempts to get at it)* Yes, but it lacks commitment, commandments, and all that depressing wrath of God! It's less filling!

BUTCH: *(Bud finally gets a grip on the Bible, which is caught in a tug-of-war between them)* Feels great!

BUD: Less filling!

BUTCH: Feels great!

BUD: Less filling!

BUTCH: Feels great!

BUD: Less filling!

BUTCH: *(they stop fighting over the Bible and turn to audience)* Gospel Lite—

BUD: —it's guaranteed not to change you.

RADIO DRAMAS

With a microphone, a couple of tape decks, and a little creativity, youth groups can produce fascinating radio programs (whether or not they're ever actually broadcast on the radio) that incorporate adventure, comedy, and drama. After all, once upon a time this was the ultimate family entertainment.

Radio dramas can be perfect for teens who normally shy away from being on stage—but just may excel behind a microphone. Goofs are corrected easily, and copies of the finished tape can be given to each participant. Almost any script can be

THE PROBLEM WITH
Friends

Hey. My name's Joel. I'd say I'm a pretty good friend—but not with just anybody. In fact, I have very few friends...*(on second thought, defensively)* but it's not because I'm a jerk.

I'm just picky.

Now take Bill. I've known Bill since we were in third grade. We used to do everything together. Once we had a bottle-rocket fight in my garage, and my parents never found out. Well, one time Bill was supposed to meet me at the mall, and we were supposed to hang out for the day and then his mom was supposed to give us a ride home. Well, Bill never shows, and I get stuck at the mall and my parents are all mad because they have to come pick me up. Bill said he forgot, but I said, "Forgot? Friends don't treat each other like that. You're a jerk, Bill."

I never spoke to him again.

Then there was Eric. We were pretty good friends, and we hung around with the same crowd at school. One day Eric told me his dad lost his job and they were on food stamps now. It was okay for a while, but pretty soon Eric couldn't afford to go to the movies with us, and his clothes started to look pretty dorky. His family moved out of their house—probably because they couldn't make payments on it anymore. I think they moved into low-income housing. I don't really talk to him anymore, but I see him in the hall once in a while at school.

Now Terri and I were good friends...for a while. The problem was, she started calling me every day. I just didn't have that kind of time to spend on the phone. She got mad because I didn't call her back for four days in a row. We don't hang out together anymore.

And Karen was pretty cool—until she started having all these problems at home. Then she started to ask if she could talk to me. What she really wanted was to dump all her problems on me. I thought, "No way!" but what I told her was, *(with a facade of kindness)* "Why don't you get back to me after you get your life together?" I mean, the last thing I need is someone who's just gonna bring me down.

Anyway...like I said, I'm pretty picky about my friends...*(an awkward pause)* Actually, I guess I don't have friends...*(stubbornly confident again)* I figure that friendship is a big gift I don't want to give to just anyone who comes along. I mean, you know how it is?

END

adapted for radio drama. Teens can be creative and make up material that fits their own group.

Programs can take the form of an interview or a drama. For an interview give the questions to the interview subject before the interview, so the subject can think through his or her responses before the actual recording.

Drama takes a bit more preparation—but it's a lot of fun, too. Here are some guidelines for building a drama script:

• Set a time limit for each of the brainstorming sessions and decisions that follow—say five to 10 minutes.
• Establish the personalities of two to four characters—give them names, occupations, etc. Then give them a general setting—school, the moon, Calcutta, etc.
• Identify the key issues your characters will face. (This will determine the theme and the purpose of the drama.)
• Consider how these issues might be portrayed and resolved in a drama. Use flow charts so that everyone can see how the story line or lines will be drawn. Break the story into scenes. Think visually, even though this is a radio drama, since listeners will visualize in their minds what they're hearing.
• Now break into groups and assign each group one scene to write. Remember the time considerations, and determine how much time each scene will be allotted. Make sure the transitions between the scenes are smooth.
• Determine what action you will describe or convey with the use of a sound-effects tape. Select music and a few key sound effects.
• When the drama is written, check that the message you decided to convey is clear to the listener.
• Rehearse and time the scenes, incorporating the sound effects and music.
• Edit the scenes as necessary.
• Record.

Bill Swedberg

MATCH OF THE GENERATIONS

Perform this sketch for an event attended by both teenagers and their parents, whether a youth Sunday service or a fundraising banquet. The dialogue (which begins on page 126) strikes a familiar chord among family members and easily provokes later discussions in your meetings or between parents and their children. *Luis Cataldo*

BUNGEE JUMPING WITH GOD

A simple sketch for two characters that explores the risks of faith in terms of bungee jumping. It begins on page 129. *Steve Wunderink*

AMERICAN EXPRESS DATING CARD

Based on 1 Corinthians 13, this sketch (on page 131) can be presented with very little preparation. The only prop is a credit card. *Joel Hunt and Kara M. Hunt*

BEST FRIENDS GO TO THE MOVIES

After performing this brief sketch (on page 133), generate a discussion with questions like these:
• Can you identify with Brad? In what way?
• Read 1 Corinthians 3:16. Would you be a better Christian if Jesus were physically with you? Explain.
• Read 1 Corinthians 2, then list everything the Holy Spirit offers us. Are you limiting the Spirit's work in your life? If so, how?
• If Jesus were to visit your home, what one thing would he point out that most needs to be changed in your life? Write it on a 3x5 card, and carry it with you for the next week.

Just as your students may carry photos of their best friends in their wallets or purses—or tack them up in their rooms—ask kids to consider carrying or posting a picture of Jesus, too: an additional reminder that Jesus is always with us through the Spirit. *James Wing*

Match of the Generations

CHARACTERS
•Mom (cast an adult in this role) •Dad (adult) • The Kid (student) •Big Sister (student) •Ring announcer and referee

PROPS
•4 Standards joined by 3 cords (like those in banks to mark lines; banquet facilities usually have these available)
•2 Chairs •1 Loud bell •2 Sets of boxing gloves

The cords and standards stage left or right. Two chairs, facing the audience, are center stage. Dad is reading the paper, seated in one chair, feet propped up on the other. The Kid enters.

KID: Dad, I'm outta here.

DAD: Where are you going, Kid?

KID: Just out.

DAD: Well, where's out?

KID: I don't know, just around.

DAD: This is not going to be another one of those, is it?

KID: Looks like it, Dad.

(As the Announcer is speaking, the cast uses the standards and cords to make a three-sided boxing ring. The chairs are moved to the two upstage corners of the ring; Dad and The Kid take their places there. Beside The Kid stands Big Sister; beside Dad stands Mom. The four of them are busy putting gloves on Dad and The Kid)

ANNOUNCER: Ladies and gentlemen! Tonight's main event...the challenge match of the generations. **(pointing as he speaks)** In this corner, weighing in at one spare tire over his ideal weight, over-worked and underappreciated: Dad. And in this corner, equipped with driver's license, girlfriend, and all the right answers: The Kid. In Dad's corner will be his lifelong companion, Mom. And in The Kid's corner will be the former champion, Big Sister. The rules are...One: no cheap shots. Two: Dad, no calling Mom into the ring for help. Three: Kid, no comparing yourself to your sister. Now go to your corners and when you hear the bell, come out fighting.

(Bell rings. Dad and The Kid put on boxing gloves and move to the center of the ring, circling each other, gloves up, taking occasional, tentative jabs at each other)

DAD: Where are you going?

KID: Out.

DAD: Where?

KID: Out.

DAD: Where?

KID: Out.

ANNOUNCER: Okay, break.

DAD: What are you going to be doing?

KID: Nothing.

DAD: Nothing is the kind of activity that ends up in the police blotter.

KID: Dad, you know there's nothing to do in this town. We'll probably get a pizza and rent a movie.

DAD: What movie will you be renting?

KID: I don't know. We'll just find one.

DAD: I just don't want you watching any garbage.

KID: Okay. We'll probably get *The Little Mermaid*.

DAD: Who will you be with?

KID: You know, John, Joe, Jack.

DAD: John who? Joe who? Jack who? Do I know these guys?

KID: Yeah, Dad. You met them when you made me do Cub Scouts.

DAD: Well, how can I remember that long ago? Have I met their parents?

KID: They were at the last football game. I think you saw them there.

DAD: I don't remember. Well, whose house are you going to?

KID: Probably Joe's house.

DAD: Are his parents going to be home?

KID: I don't know.

DAD: You know, we finished the game room so we could have people over. Why don't you all come here?

KID: Because you guys are always here.

DAD: Well, what did your mother say about all this?

KID: She said it was okay with her if it was okay with you.

(Bell rings. Dad and The Kid go to their respective corners)

MOM: *(to Dad)* Remember to ask more questions. When will he be home? Has he done his homework? What about cleaning up his room? Just keep asking questions, and try to be fair.

SISTER: *(to The Kid)* You did a great job. You really danced around those questions. Just remember, be vague. When he asks about what time you'll be home, he'll probably insist on getting specific, so shoot for one o'clock and settle for midnight. Just try to get out the door as soon as possible.

(Bell rings; Dad and The Kid return to the ring as before)

KID: Dad, I gotta go.

DAD: Just a minute. I have some more questions. When will you be home?

KID: When the movie's over. Probably late.

DAD: When's late?

KID: I don't know. Maybe one o'clock.

DAD: One o'clock! That's too late. You be home by 10:30.

KID: 10:30! None of my friends have to be home by 10:30.

DAD: Well, if all your friends drove off a cliff, would you follow them?

KID: *(rolling his eyes)* Not <u>that</u> one again.

DAD: I want to be fair. Let's see. How about 11:00?

KID: But I have to take Tracy home. And she doesn't have to be home until 11:45.

DAD: Okay, you can be home at 11:45, too.

KID: But I have to drive her home and then get home after that.

DAD: Okay, let's compromise. How about...you be home by midnight.

KID: Okay, Dad.

DAD: Now. Is your homework done?

KID: Dad, it's Friday night.

DAD: There's no law against studying on a Friday. Mark next door studies on Friday night.

KID: Mark's a geek.

DAD: But Mark got accepted at Harvard.

KID: I'll get in somewhere, Dad.

DAD: Well, is your room clean?

KID: I'll clean it tomorrow. I'll have all day to work on it. *(Bell rings. Dad and The Kid go to their corners)*

SISTER: *(to The Kid)* Remember to get money for gas before you leave—and whatever you do, don't get into a discussion about getting a job.

DAD: *(to Mom)* Why do we always argue like this?

MOM: *(to Dad)* I think it's that we see so much potential in him, and we want the best for him. By the way, I just gave him $20 this morning, so he shouldn't need any money.

(Bell rings and Dad and The Kid enter the ring once again)

KID: Gotta go, Dad. Oh, and I need $20.

DAD: Your mother just gave you $20.

KID: I had to eat.

DAD: Why can't you ever eat at home? We have plen—

KID: *(interrupting)* But the car needs gas, so I really need some money.

DAD: Why can't you use your allowance for gas?

KID: It's all gone.

DAD: Where did it go?

KID: I had to eat.

DAD: If you had a job, you wouldn't have to be asking for money all the time. I noticed a Help Wanted sign at the ice cream store just last—

KID: *(interrupting)* Gotta go, Dad. My friends are waiting. Be back by one o'clock. *(exits past Big Sister—and gives her a thumbs-up signal on his way out)*

DAD: Be home by midnight!

END

Bungee Jumping with God

CHARACTERS
•Instructor •Jumper

PROPS
•Rope

● ●

On a bridge or in a bucket on a crane, a novice is working up nerve to make his or her first bungee jump. To the audience's perception, the rope is anchored somewhere above the two characters, so the rope should hang down from above and be tied to the Jumper's ankles, the slack coiled at his feet.

JUMPER: *(peering nervously over the edge)* Sure this is safe?

INSTRUCTOR: Of course it is. Hundreds of people have already done it.

JUMPER: Yeah, but what kind of shape are they in now?

INSTRUCTOR: It all depends on how you jump.

JUMPER: Wha—what do you mean?

INSTRUCTOR: Well, there are several ways you can do this. Some are safer than others. Some are just plain stupid.

JUMPER: Stupid?

INSTRUCTOR: Some people jump without being tied to anything solid. They insist on tying their own cord—won't trust anyone else to tie it for them—and, of course, the knot usually comes loose when the jumper puts any stress on it.

JUMPER: That is stupid.

INSTRUCTOR: What's even dumber is leaping without being tied to anything at all—which is what some people actually do. They just jump—and on their way down, they look up at me with that See?-I-can-do-anything look. "It's easy!" they yell to those climbing up, as they fall past them.

JUMPER: What happens to them?

INSTRUCTOR: I've never seen one come back up for a second jump.

JUMPER: *(swallowing hard)* Oh...

INSTRUCTOR: Don't worry. As long as you jump the right way, nothing will happen to you. Lots of people jump regularly—every day of their lives, in fact.

JUMPER: Every day?

INSTRUCTOR: Sure. Once you do it the right way, it gets more familiar the next time, and then you go higher and take bigger jumps. That's how you build the faith up.

JUMPER: *(looking down, still nervous)* By jumping?

INSTRUCTOR: Sure. The first time is always the hardest. After that leap of faith, it's easier because you know it's safe—when done the right way, of course.

JUMPER: So I can't tie this thing myself?

INSTRUCTOR: Nope, not if you want to be safe.

JUMPER: So what do I do? Thanks to the fog, I can't see the bottom and *(looking up, squinting)* I can't see through the mist what this is tied to up there.

INSTRUCTOR: That's the adventure of being who you are.

JUMPER: Who I am?

INSTRUCTOR: You're a Christian, right?

JUMPER: Well...yes.

INSTRUCTOR: There's the adventure. Since you can't see the bottom—

JUMPER: *(panicky)* There is a bottom down there, isn't there?

INSTRUCTOR: Sure, but it's not the same for everybody. What's under that fog is different for everyone.

JUMPER: Well, what is it for me?

INSTRUCTOR: *(shrugs)* Dunno.

JUMPER: *(giving the cord a couple tugs)* Okay, so what's the top end of the bungee cord tied to?

INSTRUCTOR: Up in that mist, if you do it right, Jesus is holding the cord.

JUMPER: He is? *(looking up, straining to see)* Really? I can't see him.

INSTRUCTOR: Neither can I. But rest assured he's up there. If you saw him holding, would that help?

JUMPER: It sure would!

INSTRUCTOR: But he told you, over and over, that he would be there holding that cord for you whenever you ask him to.

JUMPER: Yeah, but—

INSTRUCTOR: And he's provided you the stories of many successful jumpers—Abraham, for example. Man, could he jump. And Moses and Daniel and Esther and Mary and Paul...

JUMPER: Yeah, but—

INSTRUCTOR: So why on earth do you need to see him up there?

JUMPER: *(tentatively)* I guess I don't, as long as I know he's there...

INSTRUCTOR: He's there, all right. All you have to do is ask him to hold the cord while you jump, and he'll do it. He promises.

JUMPER: What about <u>this</u> end of the cord? *(looking down at his ankles)* Will he tie it good and tight on my feet, too?

INSTRUCTOR: That's our job. Why don't we tighten 'em up before you jump? I'll show you how to do it. *(kneels, begins to explain to Jumper how to tighten the cords, etc.)*

American Express

DATING CARD

CHARACTERS
•Salesman •Thief •Victim

SALESMAN: You are about to witness a crime, a crime that could happen to you if you don't already own the American Express Dating Card. Don't leave home without it!

THIEF: *(casually walks by the Victim)* Hi there.

VICTIM: Hello. *(Thief and Victim freeze after this conversation)*

SALESMAN: Did you see that?! Did you see what happened?! Let's go back and watch it again in slow motion.

VICTIM: Olleh *("Hello" backward)*

THIEF: Ereht ih. *("Hi there" backward, walks backward to other end of room)*

SALESMAN: Let's change the speed setting to 1,000 times slower than normal so we can see what really happened.

THIEF: *(walks toward the Victim and pauses)* Hi there.

VICTIM: Get away from me you...you...that's what you are! Get away or I'll use my American Express Dating

Card on you. *(pulls out her American Express Dating Card; and reads from the back of it)*

THIEF: I wanna talk to you right now!

VICTIM: "Love is patient." Let's talk later.

THIEF: No! I'm gonna have it out with you right now!

VICTIM: "Love is kind." Don't shout.

THIEF: You flaked out on our date last Friday so you could go out with Bob!

VICTIM: "Love does not envy." I can go out with whomever I want.

THIEF: Well, in that case, on Monday I went out with Barbara, on Tuesday I went out with Susie, on Wednesday I went out with—

VICTIM: "Love does not boast."

THIEF: Come on now! There's no question that I'm the ultimate masculine fulfillment of every feminine dream!

VICTIM: "Love is not proud."

THIEF: Kiss me, you fool!

VICTIM: "Love is not rude." Or crude!

THIEF: Come on, baby. I want you.

VICTIM: "Love is not self-seeking." Get away!

THIEF: Listen, baby! You're really getting on my nerves.

VICTIM: "Love is not easily angered."

THIEF: Oh yeah? Well, what about that time I took you to see the *Batman* movie, and you got so mad at the Joker that you went up and punched a hole in the screen?

VICTIM: "Love keeps no record of wrongs"—and get out of here before I lay one on you. *(raises fist)*

THIEF: You would really enjoy that, wouldn't you?

VICTIM: "Love does not delight in evil, but rejoices with the truth."

THIEF: Baby, you need a strong man like me to protect you.

VICTIM: "Love always protects." You sure aren't protecting me now. *(yelling)* HELP!!

THIEF: Quiet down, baby! Doesn't your card say, "Love always trusts?" Give me another chance.

VICTIM: Yeah, well this card also says, "Love always hopes." And right now I'm hoping for somebody better than you.

THIEF: Well, my momma always told me there were plenty of fish in the sea. I guess it's time for me to do some more fishing.

VICTIM: Yeah? Go ahead. Do some more fishing. And remember, "Love always perseveres." I'm sure you'll find a shark or a tuna that'll kiss you.

THIEF: Woman, you are really cruel.

VICTIM: At least I'm not so yellow.

SALESMAN: There you have it! So get the American Express Dating Card and remember: Don't leave home without it!

END

Best Friends Go to the Movies

CHARACTERS

•Brad •Jesus •Friend 1 •Friend 2

Setting: A movie theater. (Choose an R-rated movie and make a sign that the audience can see.) Brad and two friends walk into a movie theater with popcorn and paper cups filled with water. They seat themselves. A fourth person comes in and sits next to Brad. Just before the movie starts, Brad turns to the stranger and introduces himself.

BRAD: This is gonna be great! My name's Brad.

JESUS: Yes, we've already met.

BRAD: We have?

JESUS: About a year ago. My name's Jesus.

BRAD: *(jumps, squeezes his drink and spills it on his friend)*

FRIEND 1: What's going on Brad? Thanks a lot! *(gets up to get some napkins)* Excuse me.

BRAD: *(turns back to Jesus and whispers)* Jesus? You mean, like in the Bible? Son of God? Died on a cross? All that stuff?

JESUS: *(nods and shows Brad his hands)*

BRAD: JEEEZUSSS?!

FRIEND 2: Brad! I've never heard you swear before.

BRAD: I...uh...only do when I'm stressed. Really stressed.

FRIEND 1: *(returns from bathroom; Jesus doesn't see him wanting to get through to his seat)* Excuse me! *(rudely)*

BRAD: *(puts his head in his hands, shaking head; looks again to Jesus)* Why are you...uh...I mean, since when have you been...um...aren't you supposed to be...? *(points up)*

133

JESUS: First of all, because I promised to be with you always. Secondly, my Spirit has been with you since you became a Christian last year. To answer your last question—yes. *(Friend 2 tries to hit Brad with a piece of popcorn and hits Jesus instead)*

BRAD: *(looks at the movie screen, comes to a bad scene, jumps and loses all his popcorn)*

FRIEND 1: Man, why are you so jumpy?

BRAD: *(looking away from friends and mimicking Friend 1)* Man, why are you so jumpy? You'd be jumpy too if you had Jesus sitting next to you! *(to Jesus)* Are you seeing everything I'm seeing? *(Jesus nods)* Are you hearing—*(Jesus nods again)* Don't you want to leave?

JESUS: Yes. But I can't without you.

BRAD: Guess I have to make a choice, huh?

JESUS: That's what life is all about.

BRAD: *(thinks for a bit, looks at his friends, then turns to Jesus)* I...I can't. Not right now. But I promise, I'll never come to a movie like this again.

JESUS: *(looks down and puts one hand on his forehead, as if praying)*

BRAD: *(moves to a seat on the other side of his friends, but can't keep from glancing at Jesus; Brad finally looks away)*

END

BODY BEAUTIFUL

Are you leading your group in exploring physical appearance, peer pressure, eating disorders, etc.? Lead into your lesson or discussion with this brief drama on page 136.

After the sketch prime the pump with questions like these:

• Do you agree that looks are everything? Why are some people so concerned about their looks?

• Do you feel that looking good—or looking "right"—is a big issue with the students at your school? Where does this pressure come from?

• Why do you think some people go to an extreme—like bulimia—to look right? If you knew one of your friends was struggling with bulimia, how would you try to help?

Before the meeting, write out 1 Samuel 16:7 and 1 Peter 3:3-4 on separate 3x5 cards. Ask volunteers to read these verses aloud, then ask:

• According to these verses, how important are looks to God? How does this make you feel about God? Can you think of some practical and realistic ways that a Christian could emphasize the inner beauty of others? *Anne Elizabeth Dodge Tyson*

EXCUSES

Have trouble recruiting adult volunteers for your youth ministry? On page 137 is a fun, creative way to get people thinking—and signing up to help the youth group. "Excuses" is a singing commercial type of skit, designed to be performed by students for an adult audience. *Russ Matzke*

GOD AND THE I.R.S.

This short skit (on page 140) can trigger energetic discussion on the effectiveness of prayer. Like just about any script in this book, it can be performed readers-theater style, with hand-held scripts. But this sketch is particularly effective if actors memorize lines—and even insert the names of your own local restaurants, etc., mentioned in the script. *Jack Klunder*

JOHN THE READY

There's no biblical point so serious that a lighthearted or humorous treatment can't put it across effectively. This one, on page 142, is about John the Baptist—and about being out of step with one's culture, like this outspoken cousin of Jesus. *Ted Faye*

THE WITNESS

This short drama (on page 145) raises interesting questions about evangelism. *Rich Young*

BUT LORD, ISN'T THAT A BIT SHOWY?

This skit about Joshua and the battle of Jericho is not just humorous, but also has a message that will trigger great discussion. It begins on page 148. *Marilyn Pfeifer; adapted from an article written by Stephen Bly*

LETTERS TO MAMA

This series of imaginary letters from St. Paul can be used as a lighthearted introduction to your study of any of his New Testament letters,or as a more deliberate window into the life and times of the apostle. (And if you have a talented thespian in your group, she can read the letters as only a proud Jewish mother can!) The four letters begin on page 152.

Discussion possibilities? Plenty of them! How might Mama have responded to her son's news? In particular, how did Paul's experiences surrounding his conversion compare with typical conversion experiences today—and just what is the typical conversion experience today, anyway? And do onlookers—friends, relatives—respond any differently these days to one among them who "gets religion"? *Stephen Bly*

THE BODY LIFE SKIT

All actors in this skit, which is based on 1 Corinthians 12, represent a part of the body and should wear a sign or T-shirt that identifies the part they each play. The reader should have a Bible. The script is on page 158. *David C. Wright*

OH NO, JESUS—NOT MORE OVERTIME!

This playlet, which begins on page 160, is an upbeat yet realistic version of the feeding of the 5,000 that deals with self-sacrifice and faith. The cast is flexible—you can use as few as three or four disciples who double as the townspeople, or fill all the roles with different kids. The narrator's lines are verbatim from Mark 6:30-44 (NIV). *Joan Lilley*

Body Beautiful

CHARACTERS
•Narrator •Katie •Sarah •Alison •Mary •Kim •Tasha •Rene

PROPS
•Makeup •Brushes •Combs •Barrettes

The scene takes place in the school bathroom; the girls are primping in front of the mirror.

NARRATOR: For all you guys who have ever wondered what girls talk about in the school bathroom, here's your chance to listen in on a conversation that has occurred somewhere at some time.

KATIE: Sick! I can't believe it! Another zit. And right before opening night. It's gonna take a ton of makeup to cover this crater. Sick!

SARAH: You think *that's* bad—I feel like such a chunk today. I couldn't even get into my best jeans.

ALISON: Just throw up. I mean, I don't do it or anything, but I know some girls who do and they always look great.

ALL: Who?...no, really?...who does that?

ALISON: You know...Susie and Denise. There's no way they stay that thin and perfect looking without purging.

MARY: I'm having a bad hair day. Uhhh...does anyone have any hair spray I can borrow? I mean *(points to her hair)*, look at it! I'm not going to geometry unless my hair works.

KIM: Everyone's been telling me that I've got a chance for homecoming queen, and my mom's taking me shopping Saturday to get the perfect outfit for Friday. You know, that's the day we vote. Isn't that cool?

TASHA: Clothes can't cover your nose, Kim. *(turning her head to the girl next to her)* Elephants don't win.

KIM: You're just jealous. My nose is perfect.

RENE: Caroline is going to win this year. She's pretty and has the best wardrobe of anyone at this school. And besides, Brad will be chosen king, and everyone knows they're the perfect couple. Don't you get it? Looks are everything.

END

EXCUSES

PROPS

- All characters wear signs stating their names
- Nervous Nell (holds large handkerchief)
- Hypochondriac Herman (holds hot water bottle and large bottle of pills)
- Society Sue (wears gaudy hat, jewelry, fur, lorgnette)
- Tired Timothy (wears makeup of "tired lines")
- Tardy Tilly (wears hair curlers, furry slippers, coat)
- Hostess Hortense (wears apron, holds cooking spoon)
- Last-Minute Melvin (wears bathrobe)
- Poster
- Telephone
- Cardboard letters

CHARACTERS

- Chairman of nominating committee
- Nervous Nell
- Hypochondriac Herman
- Society Sue
- Tired Timothy
- Sunday school superintendent
- Tardy Tilly
- Hostess Hortense
- Last-Minute Melvin

SCENE 1

ALL: *(sing in unison to tune of "A-Tisket-A-Tasket")*

Excuses, excuses, we always get excuses,
When we ask some folks to help,
We always get excuses!
(Each member sings one line and holds up corresponding cardboard letter. Song is sung to tune of "Rock-A-Bye, Baby")

E-mbarrassed to try it,
X-cuse me this year,
C-hildren upset me,
U-lcers, my dear,
S-imply too nervous,
E-xhausted you see,
S-ad nominating committee!

CHAIRMAN: *(sings to tune of "Ten Little Indians")*

One little, two little, three little excuses,
Everyone is blowing their fuses,
Putting their talents to other uses,
On a Sunday morning.

NERVOUS NELL: *(enters shaking, biting nails, and wringing hankie; sings to tune of "She'll Be Coming 'Round the Mountain")*

I just can't teach a class when I come,
I get so nervous, and my legs get numb,
Then if I were prepared,
Then I wouldn't be so scared,
But those children always make me feel so dumb!

HYPOCHONDRIAC HERMAN: *(enters carrying hot water bottle and pills, or thermometer; sings to tune of "Old Black Joe")*

Gone are the days when my heart was young and gay,
My health's so bad, may not live out the day,
Don't count on me, I hate to make you sad,
I know you need a teacher, but I feel too bad!

SOCIETY SUE: *(enters peering condescendingly through lorgnette at audience; sings in high falsetto with rolled r's to tune of "Jingle Bells")*

Every day, PTA
Brownies or the troop,
I am just so busy now,
My calendar is pooped.
Can't take a class, so I'll pass,
Ask another time.
Maybe I can work it in,
In 1999!

TIRED TIM: *(enters with slumped shoulders, slow gait, and sighs loudly before singing to tune of "I've Been Workin' on the Railroad")*

I have been a superintendent
For the past 10 years,
Through the joys and through the sorrows,
The laughter and the tears.
Now my bones are getting weary,
I just can't work so hard.
Get a younger man to do it,
'Cause I am just too "tard!"

SCENE 2

Scene opens with pianist playing "Reveille" and poster being displayed which says, "Later on Sunday mornings we hear…"

SUPERINTENDENT: *(paces back and forth, looking at his watch, sings to tune of "Where Has My Little Dog Gone?")*

Oh where, oh where, can the teachers be,
Oh why, oh why aren't they here?
It's a quarter to 10 and they haven't come in,
Oh why did they not appear?

TARDY TILLY: *(runs in breathless with coat only on one arm; sings to tune of "Old MacDonald Had a Farm")*

I forgot my teacher's book,
E-I-E-I-O

I left it on the breakfast nook,
E-I-E-I-O
With a rush-rush here,
And a rush-rush there,
Brush my teeth and comb my hair,
And couldn't find a thing to wear,
E-I-E-I-O

SUPERINTENDENT: *(still pacing and looking at watch, glances at phone; sings to tune of "Are You Sleeping?")*

Are they swimming, hedges trimming,
Did they call, did they call?
Picnicking or snoring, they are still ignoring
Their duty, their duty.

HOSTESS HORTENSE: *(enters and dials phone, sings to tune of "Reuben, Reuben")*

I won't be at church this morning.
I would like to, but I can't,
In just walked my father, mother,
Brother, sister, uncle, and aunt.
I would like to bring them with me,
But their visits are so rare,
I must give them all my free time,
So I guess I won't be there.

LAST-MINUTE MELVIN: *(enters in bathrobe, hair disheveled, dials phone, sings to tune of "Farmer in the Dell")*

Herman lost his shoe.
Matilda drank the glue.
Little Fred is still in bed.
We think he's got the flu!

ALL: *(sing to the tune of "Oh Susanna")*

Now everyone has sung his song,
And we must bid adieu,
But we are hoping that we brought
A little laugh or two.
You've seen excuses
In jest, but still they're true.
Now aren't you glad that you are here,
So we can't sing about you!

END

God and the I.R.S.

CHARACTERS
•Jim •Mike •Rob •Pete

SCENE 1

JIM: Hi, Mike. What's the matter? You look a little down...

MIKE: Oh, hi Jim. Yeah, I'm down all right. Tomorrow's the deadline for paying my tuition and I'm just not gonna be able to come up with the cash. So...school's out for me, I guess. It's back to the salt mines...

JIM: Gee, that's a shame. What about your folks? Can they help?

MIKE: No, not really. My dad's been out of work for the last couple of months, and they are gonna need whatever cash they have just to live on.

JIM: Can you get a loan from somewhere...?

MIKE: I've already tried. No luck. My credit's no good; my dad's credit's no good, and I still haven't paid off the last loan I managed to con the bank out of.

JIM: How much do you need?

MIKE: $750. Cash, check, or money order.

JIM: Sheesh. That's a lot of dough. *(enter Bob)*

BOB: Hi guys. What's new?

MIKE: 750 bucks. That's what's new.

BOB: Huh?

JIM: He means if he doesn't come up with 750 bucks by tomorrow, it's back to washing dishes at Mabel's.

BOB: Sorry to hear about it, Mike. Lucky for me, my old man has plenty of money. He just writes the school a check every year—no sweat.

JIM: Yeah, me too. Thank God for dads.

MIKE: Well, that's great for you, but what about me? What am I gonna do?

BOB: Have you had much experience robbing banks?

JIM: I hear there's big money in pushing drugs these days... *(laughs)*

MIKE: Come on, knock it off. This is serious. *(enter Pete)* Hey, Pete...you got 750 bucks you wanna get rid of?

PETE: Hi Mike, hi guys...750 bucks? What are you talking about? I couldn't afford a ticket to a free lunch.

BOB: Mike needs money for school by tomorrow or his education comes to a screeching halt.

PETE: A classic case of mal-tuition.

MIKE: *(sarcastically)* Very funny. Ha ha.

PETE: I suppose you've already discussed trying to get a loan and so on...

JIM: No good.

PETE: Have you prayed about it?

MIKE: What? Get serious.

PETE: I am serious. Have you prayed about it?

BOB: Come on, man. What is God gonna do? Drop 750 dollars out of the sky by tomorrow?

PETE: How should I know what God will do? But we are Christians, aren't we? We are supposed to have faith, you know.

MIKE: I think robbing a bank is easier.

JIM: Look, Mike—it's worth a try. Jesus did say "Ask and you will receive," didn't he?

MIKE: But I'm not very good at praying. Especially when I'm depressed.

BOB: Pete, why don't you pray. It was your idea.

PETE: Okay by me. Let's pray right here. *(all four bow their heads, and Pete leads them in a prayer—which he can make up—asking God to help them solve Mike's money problems)*

MIKE: Thanks, Pete. Well, look...I better get going and see if I can find a money tree somewhere.

ALL: See you later...Good luck, Mike...Hope you find that tree.

SCENE 2

The next day (have someone hold up a card to that effect)

(Jim, Bob, and Mike meet again)

JIM: Hey, Mike—You're looking a little better than you did yesterday. You must have found that money tree.

MIKE: Hey, you're not going to believe what happened.

BOB: Good news, I hope.

MIKE: After I left you guys yesterday, I went over to my folks house, and there was an envelope addressed to me from the Internal Revenue Service. Inside it was a check for $774.13. I made a mistake on my taxes last year, they discovered it, and refunded my money! What a stroke of luck! I just couldn't believe it!

JIM: Wow...God sure answered that prayer in a hurry!

MIKE: God, nothing, man. It was the I.R.S.! That check was in the mail way before Pete ever prayed...Thank you, Uncle Sam!

END

John THE Ready

CHARACTERS

- Narrator
- John (dressed in costume with leather belt)
- Middle-class citizen
- Tax collector
- Soldier
- Priest 1
- Priest 2

NARRATOR: There was a man who was sent from God named John.

JOHN: I'm John.

NARRATOR: John was the light.

JOHN: That's what some people thought, but I only came to show the light.

NARRATOR: Oh…sorry 'bout that, John. Anyway, John baptized many to get them ready for the coming of the light. Which is why people called him John the Ready.

JOHN: That's John the <u>Baptist</u>.

NARRATOR: Oh, yeah. Well, John the Whatever was an unusual fellow. He wore camel's skin, which had gone out of styles <u>years</u> earlier. And it smelled bad, too.

JOHN: Hey, don't knock the ensemble. This belt here? It's genuine leather!

NARRATOR: Not only did John dress strangely—

JOHN: Not strangely, just differently.

NARRATOR: Not only did John dress…<u>differently</u>, but he also ate stra—er, differently.

JOHN: I happen to like locust pods and wild honey.

NARRATOR: Yecch!

JOHN: No taste for the finer things in life, huh?

NARRATOR: But regardless of how John dressed or what he ate, he spoke a message that people needed to hear.

JOHN: Repent and turn from your sins, for the kingdom of heaven is closer than you think! You brood of vipers, just who do—

NARRATOR: You <u>what</u>?

JOHN: Brood of vipers. It means that they're all snakes in the grass.

NARRATOR: Don't you think that's a little harsh?

JOHN: You think this is harsh? Just keep listening.

NARRATOR: All right, then...

JOHN: Now, where was I?...Oh, yes. You brood of vipers—just who warned you to flee from the wrath to come? At least act like you've asked for forgiveness. At any rate, quit looking to the past for salvation.

NARRATOR: Lots of people had questions—solid middle-class citizens...

MIDDLE-CLASS CITIZEN: What should I do?

JOHN: If you have two shirts, give one to someone who doesn't have any.

NARRATOR: ...tax collectors...

TAX COLLECTOR: Sir, I was wondering what I should do?

JOHN: Don't collect any more than you should!

NARRATOR: ...even soldiers.

SOLDIER: What about us?

JOHN: Don't take money by force, or accuse anyone falsely. Oh, yeah—and don't go on strike for more money.

NARRATOR: And as all preachers do, John kept on preaching.

JOHN: Now I am baptizing you with water, but there is one coming after me who's greater than I am. I mean, like, I can't even untie his Nikes without feeling unworthy! He's the one who will give you a whole different type of baptism than I'm giving you. I baptize with water—but he's gonna baptize you with the Holy Spirit!

NARRATOR: Now while John was doing all of this, the priests were up to something.

PRIEST 1: Dang it, hardly anyone's shopping at our big temple bazaar—they're all out at John's revival meeting!

PRIEST 2: There's gotta be a way to get rid of John the Ready.

NARRATOR: Baptist—John the <u>Baptist</u>.

JOHN: Thank you.

NARRATOR: You're welcome.

PRIEST 1: What if we go talk to him, sweet-talk him? Maybe he's not as strange as we think.

PRIEST 2: You ever eat locust pods with honey?

PRIEST 1: Yecch!

NARRATOR: So the priests made their way out to where John was baptizing.

PRIEST 1: I'll go ask him.

PRIEST 2: All right.

PRIEST 1: Excuse me—John? Is that who you are?

JOHN: Whoever I am, I'm not who you think I am.

PRIEST 1: Well, frankly, I don't think you're <u>anyone</u> special—but I just wondered if <u>you</u> thought you were special.

NARRATOR: Now if John had said he was the Messiah—you know, the awaited deliverer—the priest would have him put to death for blasphemy, for claiming to be God.

PRIEST 2: *(as Priest 1 returns)* Well, what did he say?

PRIEST 1: He says he's no one special. So what do we do now?

PRIEST 2: Did you ask him if he thought he was the Messiah?

PRIEST 1: Well, I didn't ask it exactly like that.

PRIEST 2: Why not?

PRIEST 1: That camel skin smelled terrible, so I couldn't get close to him...Y'know, I got to thinking about that poor camel, running around without his skin, naked as a bluejay...it sure must be cold for him.

NARRATOR: Are you going to ask him or not?

PRIEST 1: All right, all right! *(walks over to John)* Are you the Messiah?

JOHN: No way!

PRIEST 2: Who are you then—Elijah?

JOHN: Nope.

PRIEST 1: A prophet?

JOHN: Wrong again.

PRIEST 2: Doggone, this is no fair. Okay, let's start over—animal, vegetable, or mineral?

JOHN: You're using up your 20 questions fast.

PRIEST 1: Well, who are you? What do you say about yourself?

JOHN: I'm a voice.

PRIEST 2: Never seen one of those before.

PRIEST 1: What do you do?

JOHN: I cry in the wilderness.

PRIEST 1: Why do you cry in the wilderness? Can't you cry in your room, where your mom or dad can comfort you?

NARRATOR: Not boo-hoo cry. Preach-type cry. You know, like a town crier.

PRIEST 1: Oh, I get it now. What do you cry?

JOHN: Make straight the way of the Lord!

PRIEST 2: Well, if you're not him, why are you baptizing?

JOHN: I told you there's one coming after me who's greater than me, and he's gonna baptize with the Holy Spirit and with fire! As a matter of fact, he's standing right in this crowd somewhere! He is the Lamb of God who takes away the sins of the world!

NARRATOR: The crowd got very quiet at that point, and a man moved out of the middle of the crowd and walked toward John. The priests, bewildered, did not understand what was happening. Then something mysterious occurred: the clouds opened up and something that looked like a dove came down to rest upon him. Onlookers had different reactions to this event. On that day this man gained four followers.

How would you react to this same man if he were to make the same sort of entrance today?

END

THE Witness

CHARACTERS
•Joe •Nick •Mr. Applegate (in a dark business suit, with an ominous air about him)

PROPS
•Table •Textbooks •Little booklet

• •

Lights come up on a typical student union. Joe is seated at a table, studying for a test. Nick, a super-straight-looking student, walks to Joe's table and sits down right next to Joe, ignoring all the empty seats around him.

NICK: How ya doin'? Live around here?

JOE: *(eyes still on books)* Yeah.

NICK: Where?

JOE: *(still reading)* In the dorms.

NICK: Really? I thought about living there once. What's it like? *(Joe doesn't answer; awkward pause)* Do you study here all the time?

JOE: *(concentration finally broken, gives Nick a hard look)* Yes, I study here a lot because over in the dorms too many people bother me and I can't concentrate!

NICK: Yeah, it must be really hard to study with people bothering you all the time.

JOE: Yes, it is!

NICK: *(begins talking faster, acts rather nervous and unsure)* Are you saved?

JOE: What?

NICK: Are you saved? You see, I belong to the Go with God Student Christian Club and we're sort of taking a survey to see who is going to hell. But you don't have to go to hell. *(Nick pulls out a booklet called "God Wants You!")* Right here in this little book, see, it explains how you can have eternal life. Page one: "You are hiding from God in the wretchedness of your ugly sins. You must repent."

JOE: *(dumbfounded and speechless until this point)* Wait a min—

NICK: Try to save your questions until I've read you the whole thing.

JOE: In case it's not obvious, I'm trying to study.

NICK: There are only three more pages. Now this verse from the Bi—

JOE: *(louder)* I am not interested in your weird religious ideas!

NICK: *(pause)* What's your name?

JOE: My name isn't important. Will you please go away so I can study?

NICK: If you don't listen to me, your name, whatever it is, won't be written in the Book of Life, which means—

JOE: *(very mad, he explodes)* Look! I am trying to study—or are you too ignorant to see that? What is it with you Jesus freaks anyway? Do you work on a commission basis? One more star in your halo for every soul saved? Well, I'm not interested—so leave!

NICK: *(pause, dead serious)* He said we would be persecuted.

JOE: *(resigned)* I don't believe this! *(slams book shut, rips booklet in half, throws it in Nick's face and storms off mumbling something about crazy fanatics. Lights fade, all except a large pool of light down center stage. Nick rises and enters pool of light)*

MR. APPLEGATE: *(from the darkness behind Nick)* That was very good, Nick.

NICK: *(his whole composure changed to a strong, determined person)* That wasn't just "very good."

MR. APPLEGATE: *(comes into the light with Nick)* How do you mean?

NICK: That was the best you've ever seen. I know it, you know it, and Number One knows it.

MR. APPLEGATE: That's why I have come to talk to you. Number One has a new assignment for you.

NICK: It's about time.

MR. APPLEGATE: There is a new church and coffee house which has just opened on the north side. The man who runs it has a very intimate relationship with the Enemy. He is very dangerous and could change our whole standing there without some fast action. Number One seems to think that you are creative enough to

come up with some good moves. We'll start you as a heroin pusher, but if you can't work with that let us know and other arrangements can be made. Can you handle it?

NICK: I can.

MR. APPLEGATE: Good. Let me warn you, Nick, we don't usually let demons of your standing take a job like this. If you fail...well, you know what will happen.

NICK: I know.

MR. APPLEGATE: Very well. You'll start right away.

END

But Lord, Isn't That a Bit Showy?

CHARACTERS
•The Lord •Joshua •General Beriah
•Commander Nadab •Simeon •Ithmar •Caleb •Horn player
•Curtain (person carrying card)

PROPS
8 Cards with the following words written on them:
- Presenting: But Lord, Isn't That a Bit Showy?
- Next Day
- The Second Day
- The Third Day
- The Fourth Day
- The Fifth Day
- The Sixth Day
- The Seventh Day

SUGGESTED COSTUME PROPS
•Yardstick swords •Football or plastic combat hats or saucepans for helmets (decorate with stars)

Play begins with all characters in a huddle, discussing loudly the battle at hand.

JOSHUA: All right, men, you know why we're here. We've got to take Jericho. We've been wandering around in the wilderness for 40 years and now, finally, we've reached the promised land. But, what happens when we get here? We've got a walled city to conquer. That's why I've ordered all of you to meet with me. I thought we might come up with a plan of attack for capturing Jericho. General Beriah, what do you suggest?

BERIAH: Starvation! I think we should surround the city, guard all the roads leading in, and starve them out.

JOSHUA: Not a bad idea, General. It's worked before. But there's a problem—Jericho has a natural spring beneath it to provide them plenty of water. And our spies report that there's at least two years of grain supplies in there. I suppose we could sit around here for the next three years, but that seems to lessen our element of surprise. We need to hit fast. In three years they could have the whole Canaanite armies surrounding us. Any ideas, Commander Nadab?

NADAB: Send out a sortie to bring back some huge trees for battering rams—and break down the gates.

ITHMAR: It's a worthy plan, sir—except that there are no trees like that around here. If only Moses was here...

JOSHUA: *(with irritated glance in Ithmar's direction)* Simeon, how about you? You're always ready for battle.

SIMEON: I think we should just fight it out. Surround the city and start attacking. If we barrage them long enough and heavy enough with our full weapon power, we'll eventually wear them down.

JOSHUA: The problem with that, Simeon, is that those walls are so high and wide. We really don't have that many weapons. We need another plan.

ITHMAR: I have an idea.

ALL: *(murmuring and nudging each other with smirks)* Ithmar has another idea!...This oughta be good...I can hardly wait to hear this... *(etc.)*

ITHMAR: How about we build a huge wooden horse on wheels, put some soldiers inside, then when they drag the horse into the city, the men jump out and open the gates for our army?

JOSHUA: Where do you get your ideas, Ithmar—the Canaan Enquirer? Sheesh... So how about you, Caleb? Any ideas?

CALEB: Siegeworks against the city. Then we could go right over the top. Here's how we could do it: find every basket we can and fill it with dirt. Get our men to carry them right up to the wall and dump them as fast as we can. We'd have a ramp in no time.

JOSHUA: That's great!

LORD: Joshua. *(the Lord is offstage; only his voice is heard)*

JOSHUA: *(looking around curiously)* Huh? Wha—?

LORD: *(louder)* Joshua!

JOSHUA: *(moving off by himself)* Uh, 'scuse me just a minute, men. Take 10.

ITHMAR: *(annoyed)* I sure wish Moses was here.

JOSHUA: Yes, sir?

LORD: Whatcha doin'?

JOSHUA: Planning our attack against Jericho, sir.

LORD: Decide anything yet?

JOSHUA: Well, we've discussed starving them into surrender, a full-strength attack...now we're thinking about siegeworks.

LORD: Ithmar contribute one of his—uh, original ideas yet?

JOSHUA: Yes, sir. Something about a wooden horse.

LORD: I wonder where he learned to read Greek?... At any rate, as commander in chief, may I make a suggestion?

JOSHUA: Sure! Uh, let me get something to write with...*(to his staff)* Hey, he's got an idea for us! *(to the Lord)* All right, I'm ready.

LORD: Day one—get your mightiest men together.

JOSHUA: Right.

149

LORD: March once around the city.

JOSHUA: *(writing)* "...around the city." Got it.

LORD: Take the rest of the day off.

JOSHUA: "Take the re—" What? You gotta be kidding!

LORD: I never was much of a kidder, Joshua. Keep writing. Day two: same thing. Day three: ditto. And on like that, for a total of six days. On day seven, however, march around the city <u>seven</u> times, shout—and the city's yours!

JOSHUA: *(pause, as Joshua tries hard as a military strategist to think this plan through)* No offense, Lord, but this plan is the pits—in my opinion, at least. We just shout and the whole thing collapses? Lord, I don't know...the men aren't gonna believe this. Don't you think the whole thing's a bit dramatic? A little on the showy side?

LORD: *(clearing his throat first)* Joshua, did you have anything to do with the plagues in Egypt?

JOSHUA: No, sir, I didn't.

LORD: Did you have anything to do with the parting of the Red Sea?

JOSHUA: No, sir, you did it all by yourself.

LORD: Did you have anything to do with the manna in the wilderness?

JOSHUA: No, sir.

LORD: Do you know how to strike a rock and make enough water come out of it to quench the thirsts of a million or so people?

JOSHUA: No, sir. And I didn't have anything to do with the burning bush or parting the waters of the Jordan.

LORD: You might say I have a reputation for doing things a bit differently. Still, I'm batting 1.000.

JOSHUA: *(rolling eyes)* All right already, I get your drift. We'll do it your way. *(rejoining men)* Okay, men...I've got another plan here.

ITHMAR: We're going to build a giant camel?

JOSHUA: No! And stop wishing that Moses was here! He's not, but I am. And I'm in charge. Moses disappeared up on that mountain and we haven't seen him since. I'm sure he's dead. Anyway, men, here are the orders. In the morning get your best soldiers and equip them with full armor—swords, spears, shields, everything. Have them lined up by dawn. Ithmar, you get the horn act together with your first horn player. We'll be carrying the Ark of the Covenant. We'll march around the city single file, and everyone is to be absolutely quiet. Then take the rest of the day off.

ALL: *(show signs of disbelief and amazement, some murmuring)*

JOSHUA: You heard me. The second day we'll do the same thing. Got it? We'll do this six days in a row, then on the seventh day we'll march around the city seven times. While everyone faces the city and the horn plays extra loud, we'll shout and the... walls... will... uh... tumble down. Now I know it sounds wild, but we're going to do it just like he said. If it doesn't work, it's his fault, not ours. See you in the morning. *(All sack out around the stage. The Curtain moves across the stage with the "Next Day" card. Horn sounds out revelry. Everyone except Ithmar starts getting up)*

JOSHUA: Okay, everybody up. Let's go. Get in line there. We've got to look in top shape. One time around the city, men. And everyone quiet, except for the blowing of that horn. That is a horn, isn't it? Where's Ithmar? *(Ithmar wanders up)* Ithmar, you slept in.

ITHMAR: You know what I think, Joshua? I think Moses is alive and well and living in the Riviera.

JOSHUA: Ithmar! Do you have horn number one ready to go?

ITHMAR: *(shrugs shoulder and gets in line)* Yes.

JOSHUA: *(all marching around a portion of the room)* Okay, let's go. Once around the city. Hup, two, three, four. Keep smiling! All the way around, Ithmar. Blow the horn! Okay, that's it, men. Same time, same place tomorrow. *(The Curtain holds up the "Second Day" card)*

JOSHUA: All right men. Everyone in line. Now, remember, just once around the city.

BERIAH: Did you see the way they looked at us yesterday? They hung all over the walls wondering what we were up to.

JOSHUA: *(talking to himself)* Sometimes I wonder! *(to men)* Now, here we go... hup, two, three, four. *(Characters continue to march while the Curtain moves across stage showing cards "Third Day" through "Seventh Day")*

JOSHUA: *(men stop briefly)* Whew! Well, men, this is it. This is our big day. I hope you're in shape. Seven times around the city, but keep it quiet. Horn, your big number is on the seventh lap. Then everyone turns, shouts, and watches. All right men, keep in step. Hup, two, three, four. Hup, hup, hup, hup. That's once. Keep it up. Hup, hup. Play that horn! That's twice...and three times. Four times. Five... six... seven times. All right, let her rip! Everyone shout! *(all shout)* It worked!...uh, CHARGE! men. Take the city! Ithmar, did you see that?

LORD: Joshua!

JOSHUA: *(looking up)* Huh? Oh! Go on, Ithmar. *(waves him offstage)* Yes, sir! Did you see that? It's amazing. What a great plan!

LORD: Joshua, cool your heels, and get this down.

JOSHUA: Oh, why yes, sir. I'll write it down.

LORD: Total, strict obedience to the Lord produces amazing and dramatic effects.

JOSHUA: That's great. Thank you, Lord. I won't forget that, no sir!

LORD: They don't call me omnipotent for nothing. And Joshua—tell Ithmar that Moses is here with me.

JOSHUA: *(with wide grin and then a glance toward exit)* Ithmar! Hey, Ithmar, have I got great news for you...!

END

Letters to Mama

LETTER 1

10 Tammuz, 3787

Dear Mama,

Peace from the God of our Fathers, from your distant son, Saul. Well, Mama, I arrived safely. The ship sailed smoothly out to Cyprus and we pulled in at Salami's around midday. I had plenty of time to visit Aunt Beulah.

By the way, little Elizabeth isn't little any more. She married the potter's son, a fine young man named Clypus. They're expecting their first by Purim. May all their children be boys! That reminds me, if I'm able to come home by Spring, I'll bring you some purple linen for sister Maria's wedding present. May she find a husband soon!

From there we travelled down the coast to Joppa. Then the long journey from the coast up to Jerusalem. By the time we saw the giant walls and magnificent gates, I was too tired to care. I headed straight for the Via Blanco. I recognized Mr. Benarma at once. He had received your letter and warmly welcomed me. His son, Simeon, will attend Gamaliel's classes with me.

After a day's rest I took time to tour the city. What a thrill! Mama, you and Papa must come here some day. Imagine! I stood on the rock where Abraham stood. I saw with my own eyes the tomb of King David. I even touched with my own hands the giant stone blocks of Solomon's temple. Oh, may our eyes see the day when a Lion from the Tribe of Judah reigns and rules in Jerusalem again. Perhaps...next year by Passover.

The hatred for the Romans here is 10 times worse here than in Tarsus. And there are street corner prophets all over the city. I even heard of a strange one out on the Jordan River. I must go out and see him—just for a laugh, of course. He seems to have the knack of making everyone mad at him. Just like the butcher there in Tarsus, right, Mama?

Oh, and I must mention another one. He spends his time mainly up north, around Galilee. We hear rumors of his troublesome teachings. But, don't worry about me. I won't have anything to do with such people. I'm here to learn of the God of our Fathers.

Please tell Papa the standard fees for Gamaliel's classes are more expensive than I thought. I will need to do some work for Mr. Benarma in the tent business to add a little income. If you happen to have an extra denarii or so, I know a poor, hard-working student who could put it to good use.

Give my love to Phineas, Elias, and Challa; also, of course, to Maria and the rest of the family.

Greet one another with a holy kiss.

Your son,

Saul

Letters to Mama

LETTER 2

23 Nisan, 3790

Dear Mama,

Peace from the Lord of heaven, and from Saul, your obedient and faithful son.

I hope my long delay in writing to you caused no needless anxiety. I've been busy with studies of the Mikra and Talmud. Oh, Mama, the cloak you sent is beautiful. It fits just right and I wear it every cool day.

A few weeks ago we had some free time, so Simeon and Rabin and I walked out to the Jordan to hear the preacher I told you about. His name's John. What a sight! He wore an old camel skin and ranted like a mad man about King Herod. It didn't surprise me a bit to hear later that he had been arrested and thrown into prison.

Oh, yes, do you remember the one I mentioned from Galilee? Actually, he's a Nazarene—Jesus, by name. He's collected quite a following up north. He's a primitive moral teacher, at best. He has no academic background. Just a carpenter from Galilee. May the Lord of heaven deliver us from these ignorant troublemakers!

I tell you, Mama, there's a great need for solid traditional teaching. Well, I suppose they'll arrest this one, too. So be it.

Tell Papa I certainly appreciate the 10 denarii. Of course, it is all gone by now. But it did enable me to purchase half of the scrolls I needed. Now, if only I could buy the other half...

I send this letter by Benjamin. Please tell me what's going on. He tells me nothing from Tarsus, only about Maria.

Greetings to all my friends,

Your wandering scholar son,

Saul

Letters to Mama

LETTER 3

23 Shebat, 3793

Dear Mama,

Peace from your son, Saul.

Events here have been moving at a lightning pace. I'm preparing to take a trip to Damascus on official business of the High Priest.

As you can tell, the handwriting is not my own. I'm dictating this letter to my secretary. Yes, I have some staff now. It comes with being chairman of the Young Pharisees Council in Jerusalem. Most of my studies have been suspended because of the disturbances here. This Jesus of Nazareth—may his soul be in torment forever—kept stirring up the people in the north. We all knew it was just a matter of time until he made his move into Jerusalem.

He came during Passover. First, he convinced the people of Bethany—may God forgive their simple hearts—that he had raised one person from the dead. Yes, they really believed it. Then he marched into the city leading an army of followers. He headed straight for the temple and threw all the merchants out.

Later, when I heard there was a reward for information leading to his arrest, I decided to investigate myself. But my effort was not needed. On the day before Sabbath, Simeon woke me.

"They got him," he said. "They arrested him last night."

We headed for the council. But to our amazement the trial was over. I still don't know how they did it so quickly. Governor Pilate pronounced a capital punishment verdict and he was crucified with some others that same day.

The following week Rabin came up to me before class and said, "They claim the Nazarene is alive."

Can you believe it, Mama? People actually claim that a dead man lives again. Well, we all had a good laugh. However, several weeks later some of his followers showed up around town and disturbed the synagogue services with their wild tales. Not only did they say their master was alive, but they called him our longed for Messiah.

At this point I couldn't restrain myself. The old Tarsus blood boiled. I had no idea the movement could be so blasphemous.

We arrested and imprisoned every follower we could find. We broke up every meeting, disrupted every teaching, and generally chased the whole lot out of Jerusalem.

But they only spread their lies into the countryside.

I made a personal appeal to the High Priest (we're becoming quite good friends, Mama) and I received permission to travel throughout the area to arrest all I could find. You might say I'm the chief investigator.

Please, Mama, don't worry. They're not a violent lot. Usually they don't even put up any resistance at all. I figure we'll have the whole mess cleaned up within the year. And it certainly won't hurt my status here in Jerusalem.

Don't expect me to write for awhile. Tell Maria I'm so sorry to miss her wedding. May she be the mother of 12 sons! Benjamin is a good man. Treat him kindly, Mama.

Greet everyone in the love of the Holy One.

Your son,

Saul

Letters to Mama

5 Elul, 3793

Dear Mama,

Grace and peace to you from God our Father and the Lord Jesus Christ. Yes, Mama, you read right. The Lord Jesus Christ.

I know this will surely be the most difficult letter for you to understand. Please be patient and read through all I have to say.

I'm no longer enrolled at the school. I'm no longer living with the Benarmas. I'm no longer chairman (or even a member) of the Young Pharisees Council. And I'm no longer a restless, searching young man. I've found my peace before God our Father in heaven.

Where shall I begin?

I told you in my last letter I had an assignment in Damascus. It was almost noon on the last day of our trip when we could see the outline of the city on the horizon. Suddenly a bright light flashed around us.

Mama, you know I have always been truthful with you and Papa. You must believe what I say now. It was as if the very sun exploded before us. I was so frightened I fell to the ground on my face. All I could think was, "Surely this is the day of judgement, the coming day of our Lord!"

A voice boomed forth, "Saul, Saul, why are you persecuting me?" I was petrified. I said nothing for a time, but then managed to ask hoarsely, "Who...who are you, Lord?"

"I am Jesus," the voice replied.

So, it was true after all. All my pious self-righteous deeds filed before my eyes. I could see women and children crying as I dragged their husbands and fathers off to prison. I could see the poor body of Stephen as I screamed encouragement to those stoning him. By now the tears were streaming down my cheeks. I knew I was a dead man with nothing but gehenna left to face.

"Oh, Lord," I cried. "What shall I do?"

This time the voice spoke not in condemnation, but rather in encouragement. "Rise up, stand on your feet. For this purpose I've appeared to you, to appoint you a minister and witness to me."

I was completely bewildered, so he said again, "Rise up and go into the city. There you will be told what to do."

When I stood up I realized I was totally blind. I must have stumbled around, for my travelling companions grabbed me by the arm and escorted me into the city. All the time I kept thinking, what does all this mean? Is Jesus really the Messiah? Is he even more than the Messiah?

Three days later a stranger entered the house where I was staying. I felt his hands on my head and heard him say, "Brother Saul, the Lord Jesus who appeared to you on the road has sent me that you may regain your sight and be filled with the Holy Spirit."

Mama, how peaceful and powerful those words sounded. "Brother Saul" he called me and immediately I could see again.

He then asked me, "Do you believe that this Jesus is the risen Christ?"

"Yes," I replied.

"Do you renounce the power of the world and the flesh and the devil?"

I said, yes, I did.

Oh, Mama, my heart is broken for you and Papa. How strange these words must seem to your eyes. All I can say is the truth and assure you of my love.

Greet one another with a kiss of love. And may the joy of the Lord Jesus soon dwell in each of your hearts.

Your faithful son,

Saul

END

The Body Life Skit

CHARACTERS
•Reader •Nose (shy, sneezes a lot) •Foot (wears big shoes) •Ear (wears earphones)
•Eye (wears big glasses) •Head (wears large hat)

● ●

The skit begins with the body parts in a huddle.

READER: I'll be reading selections from 1 Corinthians, chapter 12. "The body is a unit, though it is made up of many parts..." *(the body parts spread apart and begin showing off their individual talents as the Reader continues)* "And although all its parts are many, they form one body. So it is with Christ. For we were all baptized by one Spirit into one body—whether Jews or Greeks, slave or free, and we were all given the one Spirit to drink."

"Now the body is not made up of one part, but of many parts. If the foot should say..."

FOOT: Because I'm not a hand, I don't belong to the body!

READER: "...it would not for that reason cease to be a part of the body."

FOOT: Oh, yes, it would. I mean, I can go places, give senior citizens rides to church, and drive for Meals on Wheels. But I can't give a lot of money like a hand could, or cook the best dish at the covered dish supper like a hand could. Maybe I'm just not needed around here!

READER: "And if the ear should say..."

EAR: Because I'm not an eye, I don't belong to the body!

READER: "...it would not for that reason cease to be a part of the body."

EAR: Oh yeah? I mean, I can hear and understand a good sermon pretty well, but I can't seem to see places where anyone needs help like an eye could. What good is it to be able to hear and understand if you can't see to do anything? Maybe I'm just not needed around here!

READER: "If the whole body were an eye, where would the sense of hearing be? If the whole body were an ear, where would the sense of smell be? The eye cannot say to the hand..."

EYE: I don't need you, hand! I mean, I'm the most important part around here after all. That's pretty obvious. Anyone can see that without me, this body's just stumbling around in the dark. What good are you, hand?

READER: "Nor can the head say to the feet..."

HEAD: Well, I don't need any of you. I can think and reason and make all the important decisions without any help at all from you guys. I'm the brains of this outfit.

READER: *(at this point, all the parts of the body begin arguing with each other so that the Reader must plead with them to stop; the Nose moves off the side and begins to cry)* "On the contrary, those parts of the body that seem to be weaker are indispensable, and the parts that we think are less honorable we treat with special honor. God has combined the members of the body so that there should be no division in the body ..." *(the arguing gets progressively worse)* "...but that its part should have equal concern for each other..." Oh, I give up. *(Reader walks away exasperated)*

EAR: Hey, wait a minute. Listen! I hear someone crying. *(everyone finally gets quiet)*

EYE: Look, it's _____. *(use the name of the person playing the Nose)* Poor guy, I wonder what's wrong.

HEAD: I've got an idea! We could go over there and find out.

EAR: Hey, I like the sound of that idea!

HEAD: *(proud)* Of course it's a good idea.

EYE: But how can we get there?

FOOT: I can take you, I suppose...*(general agreement; everyone lines up behind* the Foot, forms a train, and moves over to the Nose)*

EAR: *(to Nose)* We heard you crying and we're kind of worried about you. Can we help somehow?

NOSE: I don't know. I get so lonely sometimes. I wish I had some friends. But who wants to be friends with someone whose greatest talent is sniffing out trouble?

EYE: Well, I don't know about the rest of this crew, but it seems to me that we've got some trouble that needs sniffing out. *(everyone looks at the Head; Head looks sheepish)*

HEAD: Well...maybe you're right.

FOOT: You just come with us. We're not perfect yet, but when we all work together, we can do a lot of good after all. *(body parts form a line with arms around each other's shoulders)*

READER: *(stepping in front to read)* "If one part suffers, every part suffers with it; if one part is honored, every part rejoices with it. Now you are the body of Christ..."

ALL: And each one of you is a part of it.

END

Oh No, Jesus
Not More Overtime!

CHARACTERS

- Narrator
- Peter
- Thomas
- James (brother to John)
- Andrew
- Bartholomew

- Philip
- Judas
- Thaddaeus
- Jim (son of Alphaeus)
- Jesus

- John
- Simon
- Matthew
- Townsperson 1
- Townsperson 2
- Townsperson 3

NARRATOR: The apostles gathered around Jesus and reported to him all they had done and taught. Then, because so many people were coming and going that they did not even have a chance to eat, he said to them, "Come with me by yourselves to a quiet place and get some rest."

PETER: That wasn't easy, Lord.

THOMAS: It was really bogus. They wouldn't even listen to me!

JAMES: John and I were luckier—the people seemed to really care.

ANDREW: Well, they sure lucked out! They had a good crowd.

BARTHOLOMEW: Wish we could say the same. They didn't listen to us, either. The whole thing went badly.

PHILIP: I get so discouraged sometimes. Are we getting through to anyone?

PETER: I'm hungry. When do we eat?

JUDAS: Relax, Pete. All you think about is your stomach.

THADDAEUS: Yeah!

JESUS: I think we just need some time to ourselves. What do you say we go somewhere quiet and mellow out.

JIM: Pete, let's take your boat and get out of here.

THOMAS: Yeah—remember that spot across the lake? They'll never find us there!

JOHN: We really do need some time just to kick back. Let's go!

NARRATOR: So they went away by themselves in a boat to a solitary place. But many who saw them leaving recognized them and ran on foot from all the towns and got there ahead of them.

TOWNSPERSON 1: Hey! Jesus and his gang are splitting!

TOWNSPERSON 2: Where are they going?

TOWNSPERSON 3: Looks like they're heading across the lake!

TOWNSPERSON 1: But I wanted to talk to him!

TOWNSPERSON 3: So did I. James said I could ask him anything and he'd be able to help me.

TOWNSPERSON 1: He already helped me—look at my foot. He fixed it! I couldn't even walk before. Now I can run!

TOWNSPERSON 3: Speaking of running—if we take off now, we can make it around the lake on the south side and get there ahead of them!

TOWNSPERSON 1: How do you figure that?

TOWNSPERSON 3: Because there isn't much wind today, and they sure don't have a motor!

TOWNSPERSON 1: You're right! We're talkin' slow travelin'!

TOWNSPERSON 2: C'mon—let's get outta here!

NARRATOR: When Jesus landed and saw a large crowd, he had compassion on them, because they were like sheep without a shepherd. So he began teaching them many things.

PETER: Hey, Jesus! Look, I thought you said we were going to get away by ourselves for awhile!

SIMON: This isn't my idea of escape—there's gotta be more than a thousand people out there!

MATTHEW: I say we turn around and go back. This is really ridiculous.

JUDAS: I don't need this. This had been a bad week, anyway. I'm tired of people.

JESUS: Look at their faces. I know we're all tired, and we do need time away—but look at these people. They need us. They're why we're here.

JAMES: They may be why you're here. I'm tired and hungry!

JUDAS: Look, Lord, I know you have this thing about helping people—but we need some time off.

THOMAS: Yeah, what about weekends and holidays? We never get a break!

JESUS: Look in their eyes—they're searching for the love and acceptance that only God can give them.

PETER: I can understand that. But what about us?

MATTHEW: It isn't gonna hurt them to wait a couple of hours. C'mon, Jesus, be reasonable.

THOMAS: Yeah—sometimes you really overdo this caring bit.

JOHN: You might as well give it up, Thomas. You know he's going to talk to them.

THOMAS: Yeah, yeah, I know—drop anchor!

NARRATOR: By this time it was late in the day, so his disciples came to him. "This is a remote place," they said, "and it's already very late. Send the people away so they can go to the surrounding countryside and villages and buy themselves something to eat." But he answered, "You give them something to eat." They said to him, "That would take eight months of a man's wages! Are we to go and spend that much on bread and give it to them to eat?" "How many loaves do you have?" he asked. When they found out, they said, "Five—and two fish." Then Jesus directed them to have all the people sit down in groups on the green grass.

THOMAS: Uh, Jesus, it's really getting late—and in case you haven't noticed, this isn't exactly the center of town.

JIM: As in, we don't see any restaurant or grocery store around.

BARTHOLOMEW: Yeah—why don't you cut it short so these people can go home to eat. They've got to be really hungry.

JOHN: Or at least they can go into one of the villages to eat. It's not fair to make them starve to death.

JESUS: You're right. Feed them.

JOHN: Feed them?

JAMES: Are you crazy? There are thousands of people here! We're not exactly rich—and there's no place to get food even if we were.

JUDAS: He's right. It would take a small fortune to feed these people, to say nothing of the problem of where to get anything worth eating.

THOMAS: Are you seriously suggesting that we dig up something to feed this whole bunch?

PETER: We really don't have enough, Jesus—even for us!

JESUS: How much is "enough"?

PETER: I don't know...

JESUS: How many loaves do we have?

MATTHEW: There's not even enough for us, Jesus, much less all these other people!

THADDAEUS: Yeah, we have exactly five loaves of bread and two very small fish.

JESUS: Tell everyone to sit down on the grass. Tom, you and John cover that area over there—Pete, you take the hillside to the left. If you all split up, we can get them to sit down pretty fast.

NARRATOR: So they sat down in groups of hundreds and fifties. Taking the five loaves and the two fish and looking up to heaven, he gave thanks and broke the loaves.

THOMAS: Okay, Lord, there's about 50 or 100 in each group. I sure don't see how this is going to help...

ANDREW: Yeah—some of them are complaining already.

JOHN: And everyone wants to know what's going on.

JESUS: So let's say the blessing and eat.

JOHN: But Jesus—!

JESUS: Father, we thank you for your many blessings on us, and we thank you for what we are about to eat.

NARRATOR: Then he gave them to his disciples to set before the people. He also divided the two fish among them all.

THOMAS: Lord—are you, uh, sure you want to do this? If we hand out these little pieces of fish and these crumbs of bread, they're either going to stone us or laugh at us—or both.

JESUS: Feed the people.

THOMAS: Okay, Lord—but this time I think you've finally done it. This isn't gonna work!

JESUS: Trust me.

NARRATOR: They all ate and were satisfied, and the disciples picked up 12 basketfuls of broken pieces of bread and fish. The number of the men who had eaten was 5,000.

THOMAS: I don't believe this, Jesus.

PETER: There was enough for the whole crowd!

MATTHEW: It's like it just kept growing and growing!

ANDREW: Yeah—the more they took, the more there was!

BARTHOLOMEW: We have enough leftover bread and fish to feed a small army!

PHILIP: At least 12 basketfuls!

JIM: Hey, Jesus—what are we supposed to do with all these leftovers?

END

AND OUR GUEST TONIGHT IS—

Call it "Oprah Winfrey," "The Tonight Show," "The Rosie O'Donnell Show"—any talk-show format will do for this interview about prayer with Sibellius the angel. Actors can read their scripts reader-theater style instead of memorizing their lines. The script begins on page 165. *Dave Carver*

THE BILL, PLEASE

Use this short, three-character skit on page 169 to open up conversation about sin, death, and grace. *Don Miller*

THE TITHER

When it's time for a lesson or discussion on stewardship, giving, or tithing, try this reading or monologue on page 172. It needs only one character—and your kids would love to see one of your church's deacons, elders, or pastors play the part. *E. Parke Brown*

WAR OF YOUR WORLD

Recorded before your meeting, this reading is intended to heighten your group's awareness of social, political, and spiritual conflict in their world. The Bible reader should read the Scripture passages in a formal manner. The news reader should sound like the typical, fast-talking, late-breaking-news anchor.

This reading, which begins on page 173, is based on Genesis 1. If your kids enjoy this, try your hand at writing your own versions of this, on whatever scriptural passage or topic you're studying. *James Vanderbeek*

CAN YOU HOLD, PLEASE?

Assigned to a student or sponsor ahead of time so it can be practiced, this monologue (which begins on page 176) suits a lesson or discussion about priorities and time with God. *Brad Fulton*

ELEVATOR

Need a jump-start for a discussion about worry? Try the skit on page 178—two girls and two boys can do a good job of this with a minimum of rehearsal, script in hand if necessary. Following the skit, use these discussion questions and Scripture references for a Bible study on worry.

To begin the discussion after the skit, ask your group questions like these:
• What do you worry about?
• What is your worst fear?
• What causes fear?
• Should Christians worry? About what?
• Should Christians fear the future?

Then ask students to read several of the following verses aloud; ask the group if anything in those verses changes their opinions about Christians worrying.
• Luke 10:38-42
• Jeremiah 17:7-8
• Matthew 13:22 (or read the whole parable and its explanation in 13:1-23)
• Mark 4:19; Luke 8:14 (parallel passages for the parable of the sower in Matthew)
• Matthew 6:25-34 (cf Luke 12:22-34)
• Matthew 10:17-20 (cf Mark 13:9-11; Luke 12:11-12; 21:12-15); Philippians 2:25-30
• 1 Peter 5:7
• Deuteronomy 28:58, 64-68
• Psalm 139:23-24
• Proverbs 12:25
• Ecclesiastes 2:21-22
• Philippians 4:6-9
Becky Ross

FACES R US

Introduce a lesson on appearances, attitudes, or related topics with this skit, which begins on page 180.

In a table top or sheet of plywood, cut four holes, each big enough for someone's head to fit through. Set up the table and cover its front and sides with a sheet of butcher paper. Place a cardboard box big enough to cover someone's head over each hole.

Decorate the table like a department-store display of faces for sale. Perhaps label the boxes according to the types of faces inside, and place price tags on each box. With some kind of sign identify the name of the store—Faces R Us.

Prepare several kids to act out the types of faces you choose to describe. They will be hidden under the table and stick their heads up through the holes in the table top. (It's even more hilarious for one person to act out all the faces by moving from one hole to the next as the boxes are lifted and lowered by the salesperson.)

AND OUR GUEST TONIGHT IS—

CHARACTERS
•Nosie •Sibellius •Modern Pharisee •IRS auditor

• •

NOSIE: Hello, and welcome to the Nosie Winifred Show! Do we have a guest tonight! Yessir, our producers went far and wide to get tonight's guest, and I know you'll be thrilled to welcome to our show a young angel named Sibellius. Yes, you heard me right—we'll be talking with an honest-to-goodness, real, live angel. So let's get started and give a big welcome to Sibellius!

SIBELLIUS: Thanks, folks, and thank you, Nosie. I want to say that it's great to be here tonight. I don't ordinarily get a chance to watch much TV, and this is a fascinating experience for me.

NOSIE: You're in sort of a fascinating business yourself, Sibellius. I mean, it's not every day that a girl gets to meet a real live angel.

SIBELLIUS: It's a living. No, seriously, it's a privilege to serve.

NOSIE: Tell me, Sibellius, what do you do? I mean, I don't see any wings or a halo. Is that stuff a bunch of myths or what? What's an angel for?

SIBELLIUS: That's a good question, Nosie. You see, there are a lot of us angels, and we all have different jobs. The halos and wings are still worn by your more traditional types—you know, your Michaels and Gabriels—but by and large we're a fairly modern lot. You asked what I do, though: I'm chief officer in charge of Receiving and Answering.

NOSIE: You answer prayers? I thought that only...well, you know...he could do that.

SIBELLIUS: Right you are, Nosie. When I say that I'm in charge of prayers, what I mean is that I act as secretary to the Boss—you know, keep files and that sort of thing. He doesn't really need me, I suppose, but he took me on a few millennia ago when the Demon Possession Department became overloaded. It's a nice job.

NOSIE: So you're in on all the prayers, huh? I suppose that you know what I prayed about this morning. *(smiles as thought enters her mind)* Do you give out any inside info?

SIBELLIUS: Nosie, you and I are both professionals! I'm frankly shocked you'd even ask me that sort of question.

NOSIE: *(somewhat shamed)* Sorry, Sib—I don't know what came over me. Could you tell us a little bit more about prayer in general, at least?

SIBELLIUS: There's nothing I like to do better than talk shop. You know, prayer is possibly the most important part of a person's life, but most of you humans just ignore it. I mean, it's actually talking to God himself. The Boss. The Creator. Mr. Big. He actually gives you a chance to talk to him, face-to-face—yet most people pretend that he isn't there. It's a shame.

NOSIE: I've always wondered about something, Sibellius. Does he really care if we pray?

166

SIBELLIUS: Does he ever! You folks just wouldn't believe how much he cares about all of you! He just gets incredibly happy when somebody takes the time to tell him how things are going. You know, he really appreciates it when you take the time to tell him you appreciate all he's done down here.

NOSIE: So you're saying that prayer is a face-to-face conversation with God.

SIBELLIUS: That's right. I guess you could say that it's a kind of hot line to the Big Guy.

NOSIE: Okay, we know a little bit about what prayer is. Could you give us a few tips on how to pray? I think that's one thing that our viewers get confused about.

SIBELLIUS: It's interesting that you should ask that, Nosie. I've just produced a training film for our rookie angels, and I brought along a couple of clips that you might find interesting.

NOSIE: Great. Let's dim the lights. Sibellius, do you have any intro for this?

SIBELLIUS: Yes. This first scene is of two guys praying in church. It's a textbook case of good and bad prayers. The first person we'll see is a descendent of who we called Pharisees back in the first century.

NOSIE: Okay now, if our audience will turn around and look at the monitor, we'll get started. *(The "film" is actually a dramatization in modern dress of Luke 18:9-14. In the back of the room with a flashlight or spotlight on the spot, the Pharisee adult, man or woman, dressed up in the latest high fashion, stands up to deliver a modern version of the Pharisee's prayer)*

SIBELLIUS: Okay, let's cut it right there. *(spotlight is killed)* I think we can all see what's wrong in this prayer. Face it—this churchgoer's got an ego that would put Muhammad Ali to shame. This is the type who sees God only as a cosmic pal who can hardly wait to talk to a church leader as great as he is. What this religious prayer doesn't realize, though, is that he has no grounds to make himself out better than anyone else—you know as well as I do that all people have done wrong, and everybody needs to be forgiven. Seems like the Pharisee-descendent doesn't understand this yet. Let's look at the next clip. You may be surprised at what this IRS auditor does. *(Another adult— a modern tax collector, perhaps in an open-necked shirt with a loosened tie, shirtsleeves rolled up—prays his or her prayer, á la Luke 18:13. Kill spotlight at end of prayer)*

NOSIE: Okay, Sib—what does this guy tell us about prayer?

SIBELLIUS: A heck of a lot, Nosie. You see, he realizes that he badly needs God. There just ain't no way that he can make it without the Lord. Not only that, but you can see that he realizes that he's not exactly the most perfect guy in the world. You see how honest he is with God—how he tells it straight out. That's what the Boss wants—old-fashioned honesty. He wants your heart, not some fathead's bragging.

NOSIE: Let me get this straight—you mean prayer is just being honest and talking with God? But the IRS auditor—he didn't even say "thee" or "thou" once! Don't tell me that God really listened to that.

SIBELLIUS: But that's the truth, Nosie. God doesn't care how you say it. He cares what you say, what you mean, what you feel. In fact, sometimes words get in the way, so he just looks into your heart to know what's going on.

NOSIE: We're almost out of time, Sibellius. I want to thank you for coming out—er, down—tonight. And before you leave, Sib, I wonder if our studio audience has some questions. How about it, folks? Any questions about prayer? *(Sibellius responds to questions)*

NOSIE: Once again, thanks for coming. C'mon, folks—let's hear it for Sibellius!

END

The Bill, Please

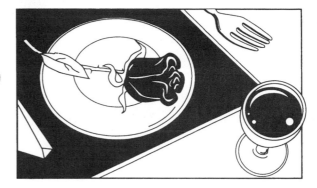

CHARACTERS
•Diner 1 •Diner 2 •Waiter

PROPS
•2 Tables (identical—with tablecloths, candles, flowers, clutter of dishes on them) •Large napkins
•Order pad and pencil •Menu •Small card (business card would do) •Background music

---

In this intimate, elegant cafe stand two tables, identical down to their candles, flowers, and draping tablecloths. Both tables have a clutter of dishes on them. A single diner is seated at each table. Diner 2 is evidently finishing off his dessert when Diner 1 snaps his fingers for the waiter, wiping his mouth with a large napkin while the waiter strides toward him, cloth over arm. Soft dinner music plays during the entire skit.

DINER 1: Waiter, let me thank you. That was the best-tasting life I've ever had. Everything was cooked to perfection. My compliments to the creator.

WAITER: Will there be anything else, sir **(madam)**?

DINER 1: No, that will be all, thank you. Just the bill, please.

WAITER: Certainly. *(takes out his order pad)* Now let me see...what did you have? Honey-glazed gossip, sweet-and-sour lusting, one large order of premarital sex—

DINER 1: Yes—and it all tasted so very good!

WAITER: —chocolate-covered lies, sautéed swearing, smoked marijuana, spicy greed (well done), vanity á la carte, stewed envy and hatred, and the catch of the day—sel-fish. Dessert? Mmm...orange-glazed disobedience and, to top off the meal, cherry-flavored disobedience to God and his Word.

DINER 1: And, believe me, it was all very, very good. Now what does that come to?

WAITER: Let me see...six carry the six plus six equals...your bill comes to death.

DINER 1: Death! There must be some mistake, young man! *(grabs menu)*

WAITER: No, sir. It's all here in blood and white. Death. You see, sir, at this restaurant, the penalty for sin is death.

DINER 1: *(furious)* But it's not my fault! I couldn't stop eating! It all tasted so good at the time. Please—can't I do something else?

169

WAITER: Sorry, sir, but your meal is over. You must pay the price now. This way, sir.

DINER 1: No! This isn't fair! I'm sorry! I didn't mean it! Please forgive me!

WAITER: *(sighs with some pity for the Diner)* If only you had asked for forgiveness while you were still eating, things would have been different. It's much too late now. Your meal is over. *(Waiter begins urging, then pulling, finally pushing Diner 1 to exit; the Diner screams as he disappears out the door. Waiter brushes himself off, returns to table, and begins clearing it. Diner 2 has observed the entire scene)*

DINER 2: Problems?

WAITER: Oh, no. Happens all the time here. They eat and eat and eat—and before they know it, their meals are over. It's all finished and they didn't even have grace. Can I get you anything else?

DINER 2: No, I guess I'm finished as well.

WAITER: Did you enjoy your meal?

DINER 2: Well, yes. All in all, it was pretty good. Mind you, there were times when I hit gristle and I didn't think I'd ever get through it. But here I am. It all seemed so fast, though…it seems like only yesterday that you showed me to my table. I guess it's time for my bill?

WAITER: Yes, it's time. For most people, the end of their meal comes suddenly. They never expected that they would have to stop eating so soon. Well, enough chitchat. Let's see, what did you have? *(glances at the dishes on the table, surprised by what he concludes about Diner 2's meal)* Well, I see you ordered our low-cal, low-sin spe-

cial: one small order of patience, one scoop of vanilla kindness, and gingerbread love cake, with obedient icing. (disappointed) Oh, no—I see you sampled from the bar.

DINER 2: It was awful.

WAITER: You also had a spoonful of lies and self-importance.

DINER 2: Yes, and I'm ashamed of it. It was so easy to taste it. It was right there on my table.

WAITER: You also had a small slice of greed. *(encouraged)* Ah, but I see you also tried the good deeds.

DINER 2: I did try to eat the right foods. I just couldn't depend on myself to make the right choices, that's all.

WAITER: *(consolingly)* Listen, sir. People come in here day after day and no one has ever had a good balanced diet. Except one man, only one—the chef's son. He was an extraordinary diner, he was, that son of the master chef. The other chef that works here is awful, though. His food always gives heartburn.

DINER 2: What does my bill come to?

WAITER: *(pauses)* I'm sorry, sir—but it all adds up the same—death. It doesn't matter if you ordered the large helping of sin or the small sampler. Sin is sin, and the bill is the same. *(approaches Diner 2 to escort him to the same door Diner 1 exited by)*

DINER 2: Wait—I have a card.

WAITER: I'm sorry, sir. We don't take Visa, MasterCard, or—

DINER 2: But this card is different. *(hands card to Waiter)*

WAITER: *(reads aloud)* "Salvation Card. Dear retailer: The holders of this card have had their meals paid for by me. Consult reservation book. Let them enter into my dining room for all eternity." And it's signed by the master chef's son himself. (examines it closely) Yes, it's legitimate, all right. Where did you get this card?

DINER 2: It was given to me when I invited the master chef's son to my table. I let him choose what food I was to eat. There were times when I didn't listen to him and chose what I thought looked good. But none of the other chef's food tasted as good. It was when I let the son choose from the menu that my food was given flavor. He ordered things for me that were really worth tasting. He told me that I was to tell others of his plan for their meal. He even said that I was the salt of the table.

WAITER: *(ushering Diner 2 out of his chair)* Well, you are expected to sit at the son's table now. *(pointing)* Enter through that narrow door over there.

DINER 2: *(takes a couple steps in that direction, then stops and turns around)* Aren't you coming?

WAITER: I will be there soon, I hope, but right now there are many more bills that I have to add up. Oh, I do hope they have their card. They shouldn't leave their tables without it.

END

The Tither

A monologue about giving

An individual is seated in church, holding his offering envelope and waiting patiently for the plate to arrive at his pew. The room's only light is on him. A recording of your church's pastor is heard, but this fades out as another recording—individual's thoughts—fades in.

PASTORAL VOICE: ...and now let us worship the Lord with our tithes and our offerings.

THE TITHER: It feels good to be tithing as the Lord commands. *(holds up a plump offering envelope)* What a dummy I am! I almost forgot the boat payment due this week! I'd better take a little of this to cover that check. A bad check would really disgrace the Lord. *(takes a few bills out of the envelope, puts them in his pocket, and closes the envelope again)*

There—now I'm ready. Oh, no—I just remembered that we're going to visit my mom this weekend, and that means eating out. Well, it's only a few bucks more—and the Bible does say for us to honor our parents. *(removes a few more bills from the envelope)*

Whoops! Did I give Janice money for the kids to buy snacks after school this week? Hmmm, I don't think so. Well, that's about four dollars—but this is food for my family, after all. *(more bills go from envelope to pocket)* And I wanted to send 10 dollars to my radio pastor so I could get that special study guide he wrote and is giving away free in return for a donation. *(he takes out more money, pockets it, then peers into the envelope)* There's still some left...well, at least one. *(he fishes the last bill out of the envelope and ponders it a moment before returning it. Then he slaps his forehead with his hand)*

Tomorrow is Monday! I promised the paperboy I'd leave 90 cents for him out in the mailbox. *(he stands and announces loudly to the congregation—the audience—as he exits)* Hey! Has anybody here got change for a dollar?!

END

War of Your World

★ ☆ ★ ☆ ★ ☆ ★ ☆ ★ ☆ ★ ☆ ★ ☆ ★ ☆ ★

BIBLE READER: In the beginning, when God created the universe, the earth was formless and desolate. The raging ocean that covered everything was engulfed in total darkness, and the power of God was moving over the water. Then God commanded, "Let there be light"—and the light appeared. God was pleased with what he saw. Then he separated the—

NEWS READER: ...and more WPC music after these headlines. The so-called Star Wars laser project proceeds on schedule. Today the developers of the anti-missile satellite—a spacecraft that would use a laser, which produces a very narrow beam of intense light to destroy an enemy nuclear ICBM—said that their latest tests have proved that it is possible to generate enough power from a laser to accomplish the assigned task.

BIBLE READER: ...and the light appeared. God was pleased with what he saw. Then he separated the light from the darkness, and he named the light Day and the darkness Night. Evening passed and morning came—that was the first day.

Then God commanded, "Let there be a dome to divide the water and to keep it in two separate places"—and it was done. So God made the dome, and it separated the water under it from the water above it. He named the dome Sky—

NEWS READER: Protesters held a rally today at the landfill site in East Brunswick Township where refuse from several northern New Jersey communities is to be dumped. Several people tried to block the road, causing a short delay of the trucks delivering the trash. Twelve people were arrested on trespassing charges. Also State Highway 18 was tied up for hours. The protesters were not only complaining about the garbage from other counties, but also the possible pollution of the groundwater supply used by the nearby towns.

BIBLE READER: ...and so evening passed and morning came—that was the second day.

Then God commanded, "Let the water below come together in one place so that the land will appear," and it was done. He named the land Earth, and the water which had come together he named Sea. And God was pleased with what he saw...

NEWS READER: Yesterday three large corporations were fined more than 1.4 million dollars for dumping untreated and toxic waste into the Ohio River. Investigators proved that the three as yet unnamed companies have dumped 2.4 million gallons of untreated waste and toxic chemicals in the river over the last 15 years.

BIBLE READER: …Then he commanded, "Let the earth produce all kinds of plants, those that bear grain and those that bear fruit"—and it was done…

NEWS READER: Reports from the famine-stricken areas of Ethiopia state that at least three food convoys have been attacked by rebel forces within the last week. One such convoy is said to have been completely destroyed. A rebel spokesman claimed that the convoys were secretly carrying weapons and ammunition for government forces to put down the rebellion.

BIBLE READER: …So the earth produced all kinds of plants, and God was pleased with what he saw. Evening and morning came—that was the third day.

Then God commanded, "Let lights appear in the sky to separate day from night and to show the time when days, years, and religious festivals begin; they will shine in the sky to give light to the earth"—and it was done. So God made the two larger lights, the sun to rule over the day and the moon to rule over the night; he also made the stars.

NEWS READER: In a report released earlier this week, a researcher at the University of Miami (Florida) shows that overexposure to the sun not only can increase the chance of skin cancer, but also may be related to other types of cancer.

BIBLE READER: …He placed the lights in the sky to shine on the earth, to rule over the day and the night, and to separate the light from darkness. And God was pleased with what he saw. Evening passed and morning came—that was the fourth day.

Then God commanded, "Let the water be filled with many kinds of living beings, and let the air be filled with birds." So God created the great sea monsters, all kinds of creatures that live in the water, and all kinds of birds…

NEWS READER: The U.S. Navy had to intervene when a Greenpeace protest almost got out of hand today. The demonstration was arranged to draw attention to the over-harvesting of whales in the North Pacific Ocean by Japan. The small fleet of protest vessels were blocking the harbor entrance at the home port of the Japanese whaling fleet. The Navy ordered the boats to leave, which caused a shouting match; however, the protesters eventually backed off and allowed the whaling vessels to pass. No injuries were reported. A Greenpeace spokesperson later admitted that the protest had gone further than anticipated.

BIBLE READER: …and God was pleased with what he saw. He blessed them all and told the creatures that live in the water to reproduce and to fill the sea, and he told the birds to increase in number. Evening passed and morning came—that was the fifth day.

Then God commanded, "Let the earth produce all kinds of animal life: domestic and wild, large and small"—and it was done…

NEWS READER: Statistics released last month said that each American consumes approximately 79.8 pounds of beef each year…

BIBLE READER: …so God made them all, and he was pleased with what he saw. Then God said, "And now we will make human beings; they will be like us and

resemble us. They will have power over the fish, the birds, and all animals, domestic and wild, large and small"...

NEWS READER: An apparent domestic dispute erupted yesterday into a tragedy in the quiet New Jersey town of Morris Plains. A man beat and then shot his wife to death and wounded his four-year-old son. A six-year-old daughter who ran to a neighbor for help was uninjured. Twenty-eight-year-old Joseph Brown was arrested several hours later at a bar he had frequented...

BIBLE READER: ...so God created human beings, making them to be like himself. He created them male and female, blessed them, and said, "Have many children so that your descendants will be all over the earth and bring it under their control. I am putting you in charge of the fish, the birds, and all the wild animals. I have provided all kinds of grain and all kinds of fruit for you to eat"...

NEWS READER: A gunman was arrested early this morning after wounding four black shoppers in the downtown area of Charlotte, South Carolina, during a 20-minute shooting spree. The man, Charles Smith, a member of a neo-Nazi group, yelled to reporters, "God told me to do it!" as he was being taken away by police.

BIBLE READER: "...but for all the wild animals and for the birds, I have provided grass and leafy plants for food"—and it was done. God looked at everything he had made, and he was very pleased. Evening passed and morning came—that was the sixth day.

And so the whole universe was completed. By the seventh day, God finished what he had been doing and stopped working.

NEWS READER: More WPC news after this message. Woodbridge Center, New Jersey's leading indoor mall, announces extended shopping hours on Sunday! Yes, now you can shop every Sunday from 10 a.m. until 7 p.m.!

BIBLE READER: ...and he blessed the seventh day and set it apart as a special day because by that day he had completed his creation and had stopped working. And that is how the universe was created. (pause)

Then the Lord God made the man fall into a deep sleep, and while he was sleeping, he took out one of the man's ribs and closed up the flesh. He formed a woman out of the rib and brought her to him. Then the man said, "At last, here is one of my own kind—bone taken from my bone and flesh from my flesh. Woman is her name because she was taken out of man."

NEWS READER: A man was arraigned today for sexually abusing children at the day-care facility where he was working. Later reports indicated that he may have also been sexually abusing his daughter, now nine, for the last four years.

BIBLE READER: ...and that is why a man leaves his father and mother and is united with his wife and they become one.

The man and the woman were both naked, but they were not embarrassed. May God add to our understanding of the reading from his Word.

NEWS READER: And those are the headlines from the WPC newsroom. Good night.

E N D

Can You Hold, Please?

A man or woman is seated at an office desk covered with paperwork, which obviously consumes the worker's time. A telephone and calculator are on the desk; a wall calendar hangs conspicuously within arm's reach. The phone rings.

Hello, Nancy speaking...Jesus? Jesus who?...uh huh...*(phone rings)* Can you hold please? *(switches lines)* Hello, Nancy speaking...Oh, hi honey...Sure, what do you need?...uh huh...yeah, I'll pick it up. White or whole wheat?...Okay...right, and four rolls of pastel blue two-ply... Sure, I'll run by there...oh, I forgot about that...yes, I'll meet you at the restaurant at, oh, say eight tonight...okay, see you then...*(crosses Monday off calendar)*...bye-bye, sweetheart. *(returns to the original call)* Thanks for holding. Okay, how can I help you?...Are you looking for a donation?...What's the cause? *(phone rings)* Sorry, can you hold again? *(switches lines)* Hello...yes sir...yes sir...of course, Mr. Jones...Thursday?...Sure, I don't see why not. How late do you think it will run?...uh huh...okay, Thursday it is. *(crosses Thursday off the calendar and returns to first caller)* Thanks for waiting. Now what did you say you wanted?...*(cradles the receiver on her shoulder, occupies herself with paperwork as she listens, obviously apathetic about the call)*...uh huh...and this is for which cause? *(phone rings)*

I'm sorry, can you hold please? *(switches lines)* Hello, Nancy here. How are you, Sue?...Really? Great! So you're joining the health club, too?...Yeah, gotta take some pounds off, as usual...I'd love to give you a ride on Tuesday...okay...*(crosses Tuesday off)*...Bye. *(returns to original call)* All right now, what is it you're wanting?...*(writes memos and notes obviously unrelated to her conversation, punches calculator keys)*...Gee, I don't know...yeah...well, I'd rather not get involved right now...*(phone rings)*...Can you hold please? *(switches lines)* Hello?...Hi, Tom...yeah, I thought the kids responded well to my lesson last Sunday...sure, we'd better get down to planning that retreat......Friday night's open...Okay, Tom, see you Friday *(returns to first call)* Hello? You know, I just don't think I...yes, I know, but...That's true, but...of course...I understand, but I still don't want...*(phone rings)* I'm sorry, can you hold please? *(switches lines)* Hello, Nancy speaking...Hi, Miriam...it is?...where is it showing?...all right, I'll get the tickets for...let's see...*(studies calendar and crosses off Wednesday)*...for Wednesday...okay, bye. *(returns to first call)* Yeah, I'm back...yes I know it doesn't require much time, but I...I know that...look, I'd rather...no, you're not asking too much, it's just that I...*(phone rings)* Can you hold please? *(switches lines)* Hello, Nancy here...hi, honey...oh, no, I forgot all about it...yes, I remember now...Brian's weekend soccer tournament...*(crosses off Saturday and Sunday on the calendar)*...yeah...make sure he finishes his homework as soon as he gets home from practice tonight...okay...bye bye, honey. *(returns to original call)* Look, I've— *(aloud but to herself)* Funny, he hung up...*(looking at calendar)*...oh well, I was too busy anyway. *(hangs up phone, puts on coat, and walks out, briefcase in hand)*

END

Elevator

CHARACTERS
•Woman 1 •Woman 2 •Man 1 •Man 2

Woman 1 and Men 1 and 2 huddle together as if in an elevator. Woman 2 steps among the three and turns as if getting into an elevator.

WOMAN 2: Good morning.

MAN 1: Good morning.

WOMAN 2: Nice weather we're having. **(looks beside her at Woman 1, who is clutching her purse in obvious terror)** You seem to be a bit frightened.

WOMAN 1: (afraid and suspicious) What makes you say that?

WOMAN 2: Well, you're clutching that purse as if it were your salvation.

MAN 2: She's right, you know. I noticed that when you got in.

WOMAN 1: Really? **(all nod)** Well, I guess I am a little afraid. I'm just not used to elevators.

WOMAN 2: You needn't worry. I ride on them all the time, and nothing has ever happened to me.

WOMAN 1: But what if it gets stuck?

MAN 2: Yeah. You know, I heard of a bunch of people being stuck in an elevator like this one for hours before anyone even knew they were there.

WOMAN 1: (gasping and clutching her purse more tightly) Really?

MAN 1: Yeah, it's true. I read about it in the *Daily Post*. It sounded awful.

MAN 2: Just terrible. I once saw this movie where the cable broke, and the elevator dropped all the way to the bottom of the building.

WOMAN 1: Really? **(growing more nervous with every anecdote, beginning to look around as if for a way to escape)**

WOMAN 2: Oh, that's just in the movies.

MAN 1: But it could really happen.

WOMAN 2: Maybe. But it doesn't worry me.

WOMAN 1: It doesn't?

WOMAN 2: Of course not. I've got the peace that passes understanding.

MAN 2: What?

WOMAN 2: Jesus lives in me. He gives me strength and assures me that he'll care for me and that I'll always be in his sight.

WOMAN 1: Sounds wonderful.

WOMAN 2: It is wonderful. He takes all my anxiety away. I'm never afraid, never worry about anything.

WOMAN 1: That sounds so good, I'm going to try it. What do I have to do?

WOMAN 2: Just close your eyes and ask God to comfort you. Then believe in your heart that he controls your world and trust him to take care of you. He'll never fail you or let you down.

WOMAN 1: That's it?

WOMAN 2: Just believe. Faith is the key.

WOMAN 1: Well, if you say so.

WOMAN 2: Trust me—or rather, trust God. That's what I do. **(everyone is jostled a bit as if the elevator has just stopped. Woman 2 clutches at the arm of Woman 1)** What happened?

WOMAN 1: **(calmly, now)** I don't know, but it sure feels good to just trust.

MAN 1: That's nice.

MAN 2: Yeah, that's nice—because I think we're stuck.

WOMAN 2: **(frantically)** Stuck?

MAN 2: Stuck.

WOMAN 2: **(hysterically)** We're stuck! Oh, God, we're all going to die! Get me out of here! I think I'm going to be sick...Help! **(lights down)**

END

The action begins as a salesperson dusts off the boxes on the table as a customer comes in. The skit can run something like this:

"I'm interested in buying a new face. The one I have now is really worn out, and...well, people have been making fun of me lately."

"You've come to the right place—we've got several great faces for you to choose from."

The salesperson describes each face one at a time, lifting a box to reveal the actor underneath. To keep it simple the actors may attempt to hold a freeze-frame expression that looks like the face that the salesman is describing. For a more elaborate skit, actors can wear makeup,   wigs, glasses, or other props that enhance their characters.

The salesperson can start his description of the different faces with lines like these:

• "Here's our Intimidator model, which, as you can see, is the face of someone you wouldn't want to mess with..."
• "This is our Professorial model...extremely intelligent-looking. Everyone will think you graduated summa cum laude or are a Mensa member. They'll flock to you for advice..."
• "Here we have our Playboy model, which girls find irresistible. Notice the enticing eyes. You can see why this is a most popular face..."
• "This face just might get you on the cover of Rolling Stone. It's our Heavy-metal model, complete with make-up, hair dye, nose ring, and tattoos..."
• "I'm sure you recognize the Born-again model. Notice

that the smile is permanent, regardless of how you feel on the inside...the perfect expression to fool people into thinking you have no problems..."

Depending on the direction you want to take, the final face may be that of a street person, a Third World refugee, Christ himself—in short, an undesirable face. The salesman can conclude along these lines:

• "Well, that's all the popular models...what? None of these are exactly what you're looking for? That's funny...they fit everybody else. Well, there is a discounted face here somewhere...let me see if I can find it...ah, yes, here it is. We don't sell many of these, for, uh, obvious reasons. It's the cheapest face we carry...though the few who've bought these have told me later that it was the most expensive purchase they ever made. Can't figure it out...." *Danny Greer*

THE BALLAD OF LUKE WARM

One of many effective ways for young people to get involved in learning is to let them create a drama or a video project. This script was used by one youth group for a silent video that they produced and showed to the entire congregation of the church—with excellent results. You can adapt it any way you want—go ahead and use sound, or make it a slide show instead of a video, or simply forget the cameras altogether and just make it a live drama. This sort of thing is especially fun for kids at camps and retreats. The script begins on page 181. *Dick Gibson*

The Ballad of Luke Warm

CHARACTERS

•Luke Warm •Church Congregation •Deacon 1 •Deacon 2 •Preacher •Sheriff •Bandits •Judge •Bailiff •Witness, church member •Jury

SCENE 1
At church

SIGNBOARD: As our story opens, we look in on Sunday services at the local church.

ACTION: Congregation is singing, sincerely but timidly, except for Luke Warm, who is bellowing full voice. Everyone quiets as Luke finishes the song. All applaud Luke.

SIGNBOARD: Next the offering is passed.

ACTION: Everyone puts their money in the plate as it is passed to them. When the offering comes to Luke, he puts in so much that the Deacon needs help to carry it off. Everyone stares in awe.

SIGNBOARD: The Sunday sermon.

ACTION: The Preacher is speaking. All are listening politely while Luke furiously takes notes. Camera pans back to Preacher who mouths a sentence forcefully.

SIGNBOARD: "Yes, only one is perfect and we should all try to be like him. And that man is..."

ACTION: Everyone points to Luke.

SIGNBOARD: "Luke Warm!"

ACTION: The Preacher looks confused. Camera zooms on Luke's face, who gives his most humble and angelic expression.

SCENE 2
The holdup

SIGNBOARD: When church is over, the congregation greets the Preacher on its way home.

ACTION: People shake Preacher's hand and walk away. When Luke comes out, the Preacher pats him on the back. The Sheriff comes out behind Luke.

SIGNBOARD: Meanwhile, just down the road...

ACTION: Bandits mount their "horses" and ride toward the church shooting at everyone. The Preacher and several others fall to the ground. The Sheriff tries to return fire and is shot in the leg. Luke, who sees all of this, is asked to help but he walks away. Bandits ride off.

SCENE 3
The courtroom

SIGNBOARD: Several days later Luke goes on trial for being a Christian.

ACTION: The Judge calls the court to order. Luke is brought in by the Bailiff.

SIGNBOARD: First witness—the Sheriff.

ACTION: The Sheriff, limping, is helped to the witness stand and pantomimes action of the shooting.

SIGNBOARD: Second witness—a church member.

ACTION: The church member pantomimes Luke's actions at church. The Judge turns to Luke and asks if he has anything to say.

SIGNBOARD: "Do you have anything to say?"

ACTION: Luke hangs his head sorrowfully. The Judge asks the jury for its verdict.

SIGNBOARD: "What is your verdict?"

ACTION: The jury turns thumbs down.

SIGNBOARD: The moral: You can't just talk the talk. You've got to walk the walk!

END

BIBLE BROADWAY

Most kids don't read or study their Bibles. There are probably many reasons why not, but one of the chief ones is that they erroneously believe the Scriptures to be dull and unworthy of their limited time.

Since most kids are incredibly creative, however, they should be encouraged to rework the biblical stories in novel ways so that the truth of God's Word can take root in their hearts and lives. Any number of approaches may be used—poetry, songs, skits, drawings, cartoons, paintings, monologues, home movies, mime—but the genius of such an approach is that the kids really dig into the Word so that it gradually changes their lives.

Assign your kids passages for interpretation in some medium. Videotape their efforts and show them at the next youth group meeting. Besides all the fun and laughter, you'll have some great discussions. And most importantly, kids will begin to see God's Word as the most exciting book on earth. The skit which begins on page 183 is a creative Broadway musical version of Acts 3 that may stimulate your thinking. *Len Woods*

RECIPE FOR SPIRITUAL INDIGESTION

Perform this teaching skit á la "Frugal Gourmet" or other TV chef programs. Your live audience, of course, is your youth group. Give your show a crazy name (Sharon's Shameful Chef Show, for example), and especially junior highers will clearly get the gist of your message.

Prepare some of your kids to play TV-studio camera operators, etc.—better yet, actually videotape the skit. Enter the room, dressed in an apron and chef's hat, blender in hand, and say words along this line:

"Just as spicy food or spoiled food gives you indigestion and even nightmares (if you go to bed on a full stomach), so can the ingredients you'll see tonight give you spiritual indigestion—and real-life nightmares."

Then, following the list below, add the ingredients to a large bowl one by one, explaining each one as you add them. Most of the ingredients can be pureed in the blender before you add them to the bowl. Break for a commercial (that facetiously advertises a sin). The concoction ends up extremely grotesque looking and smelling—in a phrase, definitely inedible. Students see, in a very vivid way, how sin can ruin their lives.

Scripture references are listed after each ingredient for use either during the skit or for study and discussion afterward.

RECIPE INGREDIENTS

• Popped popcorn with dirt sprinkled on it (dirty movies—Rom. 12:1-2)

• A cooked TV dinner—for example, Salisbury steak or chicken and dumplings (too much TV—Rom. 12:1-2)

• Shortening or lard (laziness—Prov. 13:4)

• Catsup (violence—James 3:17-18; Heb. 12:14)

• Close-Up toothpaste (promiscuity, immorality; i.e., society urges us to get close to anyone, anywhere, anytime—1 Thess. 4:3-8; 1 Cor. 6:18)

• Over-the-counter medication—aspirin, capsules (drugs—1 Cor. 6:19-20)

• Water in a beer bottle—and add plenty to moisten ingredients (alcohol—Prov. 23:20-21)

• Package of rolling tobacco (tobacco—1 Cor. 6:19-20)

• Quik chocolate drink (the fast lane—Ps. 23:2; 46:10)

• Alphabits cereal (uncontrolled speech, unclean conversation: swearing, lying, etc.—James 3:9-10; Eph. 4:29; Prov. 12:22)

• Baby food (little or no interest in growing spiritually; immature faith—Heb. 5:13-14)

• Dinosaur cookies, or anything that tastes good in large quantity (overindulgence, greed—Prov. 23:20-21; 1 Tim. 6:6-10)

• Miniature marshmallows, shelled sunflower seeds, or anything that tastes good in large quantity—say something like "I want it all" and throw it in (selfishness—Matt. 25:31-46)

• Candy bar, bran muffin (anything that can become an obsession, whether junk food or fitness—"other gods"—1 Tim. 4:8)

• Nail polish and aftershave (excessive concern for one's appearance—Matt. 6:25-34; Prov. 31:30)

BIBLE Broadway

Acts 3 in Bright Lights!

CHARACTERS

•Peter (loud, obviously a strong leader, impatient, antsy •John (very easygoing and laid-back, thoughtful)
•Beggar 1 (the one who gets healed—a real con artist) •Beggar 2 (his friend) •Townspeople

---

The scene: The temple gate, called "Beautiful," at 3:00 in the afternoon. A few grimy beggars sit on either side of the gate, looking for handouts. (Enter Peter, by himself. He surveys the scene, takes a few deep breaths, and then begins to sing to the tune of "Oh, What a Beautiful Morning"...)

PETER: There's a bright golden haze o'er the temple,

There's a bright, golden haze o'er the temple,

I feel so excited,

I can't wait to pray—

Oh, it looks like we're in for one heck of a day...

Oh, what a marvelous feeling,

Oh, what a beautiful gate,

I'm in the mood for a healing...

(He pauses, realizing his sidekick John is nowhere to be seen) (angrily) If John doesn't come we'll be late! John...JOHN! *(aside to the audience)* You'd think the guy was off in Patmos or something! *(Exasperated, he huffs and goes back out the gate, out of view. Then he speaks from backstage)* Ah-ha! *(re-enters and announces sarcastically)* Heeeerrrreeee'ssss Johnny! *(John enters slowly, eating a camel burger as he trudges through the gate)* Egads, man! We're gonna be late for prayer...(exasperated)* Anyway why must you always be eating? That's why you always have those weird dreams. You eat that spicy food this late in the day. Now c'mon!

JOHN: *(slowly)* Peter, Peter, Peter, or uh, what was that the Master called you...Rocky?

(From the background, the theme from the movie Rocky blares out. The actors look surprised, then it dies out) Pete *(putting his arm around Peter's broad shoulders in a fatherly manner)*, you're always in too much of a hurry...Yup, you need to learn to take life slowly...*(spying a flower box)* You need to take time to smell...*(breathing deeply, then scowling and looking with disdain at the Beggars)* the beggars! *(He holds his nose in mock revulsion at the Beggars by the gate on either side)*

BEGGAR 2: *(nudging Beggar 1—in a whisper)* He said his name's Peter.

BEGGAR 1: Yeah, yeah, I heard. *(He crawls over to Peter and tugs on his robe)*

PETER: May I help you?

BEGGAR 1: *(singing to the tune of "Hello, Dolly"—music in background)*

Well hello, Peter,

Howdy Doo, Peter,

Give me money, give me silver, give me gold.

(really ham it up) How 'bout some cash, Peter?

Hate to ask, Peter,

But my stomach is so empty,

That I'm feeling bold.

Please share the wealth, Peter!

You've got your health, Peter,

But I'm lame and I can't seem to get around...

So—shell it out, Peter,

C'mon and help me out, Peter—

You know what I'm speaking of,

Give me a little o' that Christian love

I'll be the happiest beggar in this town!

(with a flourish, winking to his buddy, obviously proud of himself)

PETER: *(looking sorrowfully at John, then the Beggar)* Sorry, pal.

BEGGAR 1: *(desperately)* Oh, pleeeeeezzze!

PETER: Read my lips *(slowly)* No habla munero, amigo! Comprende? *(The Beggar nods slowly and starts to slink away as John nudges Peter and whispers in his ear)* But, *(the Beggar turns)* even though we're as broke as the Ten Commandments...ha ha ha *(obviously amused at his feeble attempt at humor)* Well, hit it, John! *(John produces top hats and canes and they do a little soft shoe...to the tune of "Getting to Know You")*

Jesus will heal you,

He's gonna make you all better...

You'll soon be walking,

Thinking about where to roam.

You won't be begging,

Bothering us Christian leaders,

Because of all the beautiful and new

Things you'll be able to do

With...the...Lord. *(They bow eagerly, cockily) (Peter grabs Beggar 1, raises him up)*

In the name of Jesus Christ the Nazarene—Walk!

(Beggar 1 stands, springs, bouncing a bit, testing his ankles. He reaches down in wonderment and grabs them. Then excitedly he jumps about shouting)

BEGGAR 1: I can walk! My legs...I'm healed, I really am! I can beeeee somebody!

(Background music—"The Hallelujah Chorus"—fills the temple majestically. The actors all look a bit confused. Then it dies out) Lights please, and give me...a C.

(to the tune of, "Sunrise, Sunset," with feeling)

Are these the legs that I was born with?

How did they get to be so strong?

I never thought that I would walk,

But I was wrong...

Walking, jumping,

Leaping, dancing,

Laughing all the day,

(acting each of these out in turn, then thinking suddenly) Maybe I'll try out for the track team. *(jogs in place, then pauses, sobered by the thought)* Or maybe I'll kneel right down and pray. *(He does so for a moment or two, as the rest look reverently on, then he jumps up and the others encircle him. They*

all hug and chatter excitedly)

PETER: *(suddenly realizing the lateness of the hour, excitedly)* Whoa! The prayer time! John, c'mon before we miss the whole thing! *(They all turn and begin to try to file into the temple door over to one side of the set, but Beggar 2 blocks the way. He has felt very neglected during this whole episode and now wants to garner some of their attention and get in on all the action)*

BEGGAR 2: Wait, wait! *(He grabs Beggar 1 and, obviously proud of himself, begins to sing to him, a bit off-key to the tune of "On the Street Where You Live")*

I have often walked down this street before

Yet I've never seen you standing on your feet before

Now I want to know

How this thing is so...

(Peter, totally frustrated at the lateness of the hour, now has pushed through the little crowd at the temple door. He physically picks up Beggar 2 and carries him out of sight into the temple as the rest quickly follow. Three or four seconds later Beggar 2 reappears in the doorway to sing his last line.)

But I think that's the end of this show.

(A pair of hands pulls him out of view as the curtain falls)

END

• Secret deodorant spray (gossip—Prov. 11:13. Use this again later to improve the smell of your concoction.)

• Chocolate coins or Payday candy bar (preoccupation with wealth—Luke 16:13; 1 Tim. 6:10)

• Apple (Adam and Eve: i.e., disobedience—Gen. 2-3)

• Bread (settling for worldly satisfaction; "man shall not live by bread alone"—Matt. 4:4)

• Gummy worms coated with dirt (general smut and filth—Phil. 4:8)

• Can of beans (negatively influencing friends; bad friends are like beans—at first they seem good, but they eventually give you trouble—Prov. 4:14; Ps. 1:1; 1 Cor. 15:33-34)

• Can of spinach (complaining—everyone complains about eating spinach—Ps. 10:1-2; 1 Thess. 5:16-18)

• Tabasco or Red Devil Hot Sauce (anger and hate—1 John 4:7-12)

• Garlic powder (jealousy; people relish being near an envious person as much as they like being near someone with bad breath—Prov. 14:30)

• Foil wrappers to chocolate coins—but do not put in blender! (most heavy metal music; i.e., unwholesome music—Rom. 12:2; Ps. 98:4-6)

• Can of minced clams (involvement in cults; i.e., attractive on the outside, but slimy and gross on the inside—Col. 2:8)

• Black licorice or Ghostbuster cereal (the occult, the dark side of life—Eph. 6:10-12; 5:19-20; James 4:7)

• Pride—change the T on a box of Tide to Pr (pride—1 Peter 5:5-6)

• Can of cat food (dishonesty; cats can be sneaky and sly—Luke 16:10-12)

• More Quik (impatience—"I want it, and I want it now!"—Col. 3:12-14)

Wind up the cooking class with words to this effect: Combine above ingredients and mix. Not only does this recipe work every time, but it is sure to give anyone who consumes a steady diet of it a real-life nightmare! Feel free to add or subtract ingredients as you desire. In fact, this recipe works well even if you use just one ingredient—provided you use a lot of it.

There are some ingredients, however, you don't want to let near your dish. They'll ruin your recipe for sure: the Bible, prayer, praise, fellowship, serving others, obedience to God, worship, and thankfulness.

Of course, if you don't want indigestion and a nightmarish life, follow Christ's example: "My food," said Jesus, "is to do the will of him who sent me and to finish his work" (John 4:34). *Sharon Brober*

THE EXECUTION

This sketch (on page 187) can be performed casually as a discussion starter, or with considerable preparation and costumes as a dramatic interpretation of the meaning of the cross. It has two speaking parts, but any number of others can carry out the action described in the Visual column. Calvinicus and Georgius carry on their conversation oblivious to what is going on behind them. *Larry Michaels*

The Execution

VISUAL

AUDIO

Camera
(or spotlight)
on men eating
lunch.

CALVINICUS: Hi, George, What's new?

GEORGIUS: What d'ya mean? Nothing ever happens around here. Looks like another hot one. Nice day for camels, eh?

CALVINICUS: *(chuckles)* Yeah, pass me an olive, will ya?

GEORGIUS: Here you are, ya beggar. Why don't you get yourself a bowl and sit at the Jerusalem gate?

CALVINICUS: Lay off, okay? It's been rough enough today out there in the fields. Look at these fingernails!

People start
walking across
behind the
workmen.

GEORGIUS: Yeah, I know. The ground is so hard. Almost broke the yoke right off my ox.

CALVINICUS: What's going on anyway? What's all this commotion about?

GEORGIUS: Oh, just another execution. You know, one of those weird "prophets." Claim they got the answer to all the world's problems. Bein' executed along with two other criminals.

CALVINICUS: Oh. He's the guy. Yeah, I heard about him. They say he's God or something. Some people say he did some kind of hocus-pocus on some sick people.

A small cross is
carried in and
set to one side.

GEORGIUS: Yeah. These "prophets" are all the same. They supposedly fix a few legs and eyes and everyone goes ga-ga. Course, he's also charged with creating a disturbance, inciting a riot, and contempt of court. They never learn. If he really wants a following, he's gotta explain how come his God is so good at fixing legs and so bad at gettin' him outta jail. Uh...look...I gotta get back to the house and start preparing for the feast tonight.

A second small cross is brought in and set to the other side.

CALVINICUS: You know, George, just the other day I was telling the wife what a mess the world is in. On one hand you got those radical Zealots and Essenes walking around with the short hair and stuff, and on the other hand you got those phony loudmouthed pharisees running around blowing trumpets and prayin' in your ear. What are things coming to anyway?

GEORGIUS: I don't know, man. Why don't you ask Caesar?

CALVINICUS: I know this sounds weird, George, but sometimes I think if there is a God, I wish he'd do something radical about what's going on down here. I mean, you know, he could always come down here and zap a few Romans. Then maybe something would happen.

GEORGIUS: It'd be great if anything would happen around here! Every day...out to the fields...plow, plow, plow...grab a quick lunch...back to work...crunch the grain...the same old grind. What kind of life is that?

CALVINICUS: It sure would be great if we could all go back to the good old days of sheepherding like the Waltonbergs.

GEORGIUS: Are you kidding? I wouldn't go back to sheep for nothin'. Progress, man, progress. Oh, sure, it gets a little dusty in town with all the traffic, but this is where the action is. Of course, all this activity has made my wife nag a little more *(if that's possible)*.

CALVINICUS: I don't know, man. Seems like I just wake up, turn off my rooster, go to work, go home, blow out the lamp, and go to bed. I wish there was something more. I'm beginning to wonder about all this religious stuff. I mean, if there is such a thing as God, why doesn't he just come down here and say, "Hi, folks. I'm God. How'd you like to see a few Romans made into pizza?"

GEORGIUS: You ought to know by now, Cal, baby, religion is all a bunch of myths and stuff. Well, see you around.

A third large cross is slowly brought in.

CALVINICUS: Okay, George, see you later.

GEORGIUS: *(sarcastically)* Yeah. By the way, Cal, if you bump into some guy that says, "Hi, I'm God," let me know...I'd like to meet him.

END

Youth Ministry Programming

Camps, Retreats, Missions, & Service Ideas (Ideas Library)

Compassionate Kids: Practical Ways to Involve Your Students in Mission and Service

Creative Bible Lessons from the Old Testament

Creative Bible Lessons in 1 & 2 Corinthians

Creative Bible Lessons in John: Encounters with Jesus

Creative Bible Lessons in Romans: Faith on Fire!

Creative Bible Lessons on the Life of Christ

Creative Bible Lessons in Psalms

Creative Junior High Programs from A to Z, Vol. 1 (A-M)

Creative Junior High Programs from A to Z, Vol. 2 (N-Z)

Creative Meetings, Bible Lessons, & Worship Ideas (Ideas Library)

Crowd Breakers & Mixers (Ideas Library)

Downloading the Bible Leader's Guide

Drama, Skits, & Sketches (Ideas Library)

Drama, Skits, & Sketches 2 (Ideas Library)

Dramatic Pauses

Everyday Object Lessons

Games (Ideas Library)

Games 2 (Ideas Library)

Good Sex: A Whole-Person Approach to Teenage Sexuality and God

Great Fundraising Ideas for Youth Groups

More Great Fundraising Ideas for Youth Groups

Great Retreats for Youth Groups

Holiday Ideas (Ideas Library)

Hot Illustrations for Youth Talks

More Hot Illustrations for Youth Talks

Still More Hot Illustrations for Youth Talks

Ideas Library on CD-ROM

Incredible Questionnaires for Youth Ministry

Junior High Game Nights

More Junior High Game Nights

Kickstarters: 101 Ingenious Intros to Just about Any Bible Lesson

Live the Life! Student Evangelism Training Kit

Memory Makers

The Next Level Leader's Guide

Play It! Over 150 Great Games for Youth Groups

Roaring Lambs

Special Events (Ideas Library)

Spontaneous Melodramas

Student Leadership Training Manual

Student Underground: An Event Curriculum on the Persecuted Church

Super Sketches for Youth Ministry

Talking the Walk

Teaching the Bible Creatively

Videos That Teach

What Would Jesus Do? Youth Leader's Kit

Wild Truth Bible Lessons

Wild Truth Bible Lessons 2

Wild Truth Bible Lessons—Pictures of God

Worship Services for Youth Groups

Professional Resources

Administration, Publicity, & Fundraising (Ideas Library)

Equipped to Serve: Volunteer Youth Worker Training Course

Help! I'm a Junior High Youth Worker!

Help! I'm a Small-Group Leader!

Help! I'm a Sunday School Teacher!

Help! I'm a Volunteer Youth Worker!

How to Expand Your Youth Ministry

How to Speak to Youth...and Keep Them Awake at the Same Time

Junior High Ministry (Updated & Expanded)

The Ministry of Nurture: A Youth Worker's Guide to Discipling Teenagers

Purpose-Driven Youth Ministry

Purpose-Driven Youth Ministry Training Kit

So That's Why I Keep Doing This! 52 Devotional Stories for Youth Workers

A Youth Ministry Crash Course

The Youth Worker's Handbook to Family Ministry

Discussion Starter Resources

Discussion & Lesson Starters (Ideas Library)

Discussion & Lesson Starters 2 (Ideas Library)

EdgeTV

Get 'Em Talking

Keep 'Em Talking!

High School TalkSheets

More High School TalkSheets

High School TalkSheets: Psalms and Proverbs

Junior High TalkSheets

More Junior High TalkSheets

Junior High TalkSheets: Psalms and Proverbs

Real Kids: Short Cuts

Real Kids: The Real Deal—on Friendship, Loneliness, Racism, & Suicide

Real Kids: The Real Deal—on Sexual Choices, Family Matters, & Loss

Real Kids: The Real Deal—on Stressing Out, Addictive Behavior, Great Comebacks, & Violence

Real Kids: Word on the Street

Have You Ever...? 450 Intriguing Questions Guaranteed to Get Teenagers Talking

Unfinished Sentences: 450 Tantalizing Statement-Starters to Get Teenagers Talking & Thinking

What If...? 450 Thought-Provoking Questions to Get Teenagers Talking, Laughing, and Thinking

Would You Rather...? 465 Provocative Questions to Get Teenagers Talking

Art Source Clip Art

Stark Raving Clip Art (print)

Youth Group Activities (print)

Clip Art Library Version 2.0 (CD-ROM)

Digital Resources

Clip Art Library Version 2.0 (CD-ROM)

Ideas Library on CD-ROM

Videos & Video Curricula

EdgeTV

Equipped to Serve: Volunteer Youth Worker Training Course

The Heart of Youth Ministry: A Morning with Mike Yaconelli

Good Sex: A Whole-Person Approach to Teenage Sexuality and God

Live the Life! Student Evangelism Training Kit

Purpose-Driven Youth Ministry Training Kit

Real Kids: Short Cuts

Real Kids: The Real Deal—on Friendship, Loneliness, Racism, & Suicide

Real Kids: The Real Deal—on Sexual Choices, Family Matters, & Loss

Real Kids: The Real Deal—on Stressing Out, Addictive Behavior, Great Comebacks, & Violence

Real Kids: Word on the Street

Student Underground: An Event Curriculum on the Persecuted Church

Understanding Your Teenager Video Curriculum

Student Books

Downloading the Bible: A Rough Guide to the New Testament

Downloading the Bible: A Rough Guide to the Old Testament

Grow For It Journal

Grow For It Journal through the Scriptures

Spiritual Challenge Journal: The Next Level

Teen Devotional Bible

What Would Jesus Do? Spiritual Challenge Journal

What Almost Nobody Will Tell You About Sex

Wild Truth Journal for Junior Highers

Wild Truth Journal—Pictures of God

SO WHAT CREATIVE SCRIPTS HAVE YOU WRITTEN LATELY?

Are your kids still talking about that drama or skit you invented for last month's meeting or event? Youth Specialties pays $40 (and in some cases, more) for unpublished, field-tested ideas that have worked for you.

You've probably been in youth work long enough to realize that sanitary, theoretical, tidy ideas aren't what in-the-trenches youth workers are looking for. They want—*you* want—imagination and take-'em-by-surprise novelty in parties and other events. Ideas that have been tested and tempered and improved in the very real, very adolescent world you work in.

So here's what to do:
- Sit down at your computer, get your killer script out of your head and onto your hard drive, then e-mail it to Ideas@YouthSpecialties.com. Or print it off and fax it to 619-440-0582 (Attn: Ideas).
- If you need to include diagrams, photos, art, or samples that help explain your dramatic idea, stick it all in an envelope and mail it to our street address: Ideas, 300 S. Pierce St., El Cajon, CA 92020.
- Be sure to include your name, all your addresses, phone and fax numbers, and e-mail addresses.
- Let us have a few months to give your idea a thumbs up or down*, and a little longer for your money.

*Hey, no offense intended if your idea isn't accepted. It's just that our fussy Ideas Library editor has these *really* meticulous standards. If the sketch isn't creative, original, and just plain fun in an utterly wild or delightful way, she'll reject it (reluctantly, though, because she has a tender heart). Sorry. But we figure you deserve only the best scripts.